THE PICTORIAL
ENCYCLOPEDIA OF
DOGS

THE PICTORIAL
ENCYCLOPEDIA OF
DOGS

CLAUDIA LONG & BRITT STRADER

with the Photography of
ROBERT PEARCY

BISON GROUP

First published in 1989 by
Brompton Books Corp
15 Sherwood Place
Greenwich, CT 06830

ISBN 0 86124 547 4

Printed in Spain by Printer Industria Gráfica, S.A. Barcelona

Designed by Ruth DeJauregui
Edited & Captioned by Marie Cahill

Page 1: The German Shepherd is known throughout the world for its loyalty. *Pages 2-3:* For 200 years, the Old English Sheepdog guarded sheep in the English countryside. Today, the breed is more often a pampered member of the family. *These pages:* A walk in the rain is all part of the day's fun for this beautiful Golden Retriever.

Contents

INTRODUCTION

by Marie Cahill

Above: **For centuries, shepherd dogs have toiled faithfully for their owners.** *Right:* **The start of a lifelong friendship.**

Since man discovered fire the dog has been his best friend. The dog has helped man provide food for the table, tended his flock, guarded his home and—most of all—given man his undying love and devotion.

Modern breeds of the domestic dog—along with their wild cousins, the wolves, coyotes, jackals and foxes—belong to the family *Canidae*, a group of carnivores, or meat eaters. Fossil remains of an early carnivore, *Miacis*—the distant ancestor of the dog—can be traced to the transition period between the Eocene and the Oligocene ages, some 40,000,000 years ago. Later in the Oligocene period the *Miacis* evolved into two species, one a bear-dog animal, the likely forerunner to the modern day bear; and the other, an animal known as *Cynodictis*—the grandfather of the modern day dog.

Although the origin of the domestic dog is clouded in the unrecorded history of prehistoric man, archeological remains show that the dog has been by man's side for at least the last 10,000 years. One theory suggests that the smallest of the wolves, the Arctic wolf, is the modern domestic dog's original ancestor. We can only speculate how man and dog began their ancient friendship but it seems likely that a young wolf cub was adopted by early man. Since wolves tend to be quiet and good hunters, early man probably used them to assist in hunting. The process of selective breeding must have started then. The fastest wolf-dogs were kept and then bred together. Seeing that some wolves were more vocal than others, prehistoric man may have bred two of the louder variety in an effort to produce an animal that would bark to ward off strangers. In general, a high priority would have been placed on those animals that showed more submission to man.

As different cultures evolved, so evolved a wide variety of dogs. The different needs and techniques of the hunter led to the development of a broad range of breeds. Some hunters relied on dogs that hunted by sight, while others used dogs that hunted by scent or by hearing. The size of the prey determined the size of the dog. Hunting large game such as elk or deer gave rise to large breeds—the Scottish Deerhound or Norwegian Elkhound—whereas smaller prey necessitated a smaller breed, such as the Dachshund, which was originally used to seek out badgers in their holes. The different hunting techniques, too, produced the setters, retrievers and pointers of today.

In addition to hunting, dogs were used for herding livestock and guarding property, and it would seem that man's very survival was dependent on the dog. The trusty guard dog would sound the alarm if an intruder—either man or beast—approached. Tending a flock of sheep or goats would have been vastly more difficult without the aid of the tireless shepherd dog.

Of course, the early dogs existed as companions as well as helpers. Excavations of ancient sites have revealed the bones of small dogs whose purpose in life was most likely spending time with family members, and thus began the centuries-old friendship of man and his trusted and faithful companion—the dog. Dogs make wonderful companions because, by nature, they are pack animals and desire to be with others, either their own kind or humans. Likewise, humans enjoy the company of dogs. Dogs are nonjudgemental; they don't care what you do for a living or what you look like. As any dog owner knows, his return is marked by joyous barking and tailwagging. Who but the dog responds so?

THE PICTORIAL

ENCYCLOPEDIA

AFFENPINSCHER

With its quaint, monkeylike face and tripping, prancing gait, the Affenpinscher is bewitching. *Affen* means 'monkey' and *pinscher* signifies 'rough-haired terrier' in German. People in Germany often add an additional prefix, *Zwerg*, meaning 'dwarf' to the name — Zwergaffenpinscher. In France, the Affenpinscher is called the 'mustached devil.'

The appealing, funny face of the Affenpinscher is portrayed in paintings by fifteenth century artists Jan van Eyck and Albrecht Dürer. There is controversy over the origin of the breed. Some claim it is descended from the Brussels Griffon, while others say it is the other way around. The ancestor of both breeds may be an extinct German Pinscher. The Affenpinscher was recognized by the American Kennel Club in 1936.

Its large, dark, round eyes have a keen expression as they peer out through a ring of shaggy hair. They are set in a round apple head, topped by high, upright or small drop ears above a broad forehead, with a short muzzle and slightly undershot jaw.

The Affenpinscher's body is square, with a level back, and its tail is usually docked short and carried high. This sturdy little dog weighs between seven and eight pounds and is 9.5 to 11 inches tall. It has a shaggy coat, which is longer in some places than in others, and thus has a naturally tousled look. The usual color is black, but dark grey, black with grey, rich tan or brown markings are permissible. In very warm houses, the Affenpinscher tends to lose its coat altogether; therefore, owners who prefer a cooler temperature are in order.

The Affenpinscher is lively, self-confident, affectionate, devoted and very even tempered, but, according to the German standard, is 'a devil full of venom' toward an enemy. Generally quiet, the Affenpinscher can get vehemently excited when provoked, and is fearless toward any attacker. This dog loves its toys and, if left alone, will play contentedly with them.

AFGHAN HOUND

This greyhound in silk pajamas is said by many to be the most ancient of domestic dogs. Legend tells us that a pair of Afghan Hounds accompanied Noah into the Ark. An Afghan is portrayed on pictorial fabric found in Greece from the sixth century BC, and is mentioned in an Egyptian papyrus from the fourth century BC. The breed is also depicted in cave drawings in the Balkh region of northwestern Afghanistan dating back 4000 years.

Yet there is some controversy as to whether the Afghan Hound is the ancestor of all dogs of the greyhound type, or is himself descended from the Greyhound, and there is a gulf in its history between Egypt, where most authorities say the breed originated, and its arrival in Afghanistan, where it grew a long, shaggy coat for protection against the harsh climate. One theory is that the Afghan Hound was carried to Afghanistan from the Middle East by traders. Many authorities believe it may, at some point in time, have mated with the Saluki, also a candidate for the oldest domestic dog and a desert hunter.

The Afghan, of course, is a hunter. In Afghanistan, it is a valued aide to nomadic chieftains in their search for deer, wild goats, wolves, hares, snow leopards and, in fact, whatever game the locality provides and the hunters want to hunt. The Afghan's method of hunting is based on speed and keen eyesight because its sense of smell is deficient. The hound's wide-set hip bones make it possible for it to turn sharply and spring gracefully over the rocky, mountainous terrain in Afghanistan. Hunters follow the high-flying tail as the Afghan boldly makes its way through brushy country. The dog has also herded sheep and guarded the borders of Afghanistan.

Because the first specimens of this breed were brought to Europe from Afghanistan, the dog was named after that country. It was an English captain, John Barff, who first imported an Afghan to Europe, in 1907, and his dog, *Zardin*, was the first Afghan Hound to appear

Previous pages: An English Springer Spaniel family. *Below:* The Afghan Hound. *Right:* The Affenpinscher makes a playful pet.

in a dog show. *Zardin* was later the model on which the standard for the breed was based. Afghans were very popular show dogs in the 1920s. In 1926 the Afghan Hound Club was founded and the breed was recognized by the British Kennel Club. The monkey-faced dog landed on America's shores that same year, where it became a dog of fashion. The Afghan was accepted by the American Kennel Club in 1948 and won Best in Show at the Westminster Dog Show in 1957, which increased people's awareness of this dramatically beautiful breed. During the flower power era of the sixties, the Afghan reached a new peak of popularity as a fashionable accessory to people who, unfortunately, often did not understand its nature or its needs.

The Afghan Hound's striking appearance and smooth, powerful stride make heads turn. The sumptuous coat requires frequent brushing and should be shampooed once a month. An aristocrat from its elongated head, with abundant topknot, and tall, strong body to its gaily carried tail, the Afghan loves comfort and will seek out the best armchair in the house. It delights in lavish affection and attention, but may be aloof with strangers.

The Afghan may often seem to be looking inscrutably into the distance, and its independent and somewhat fey character inspires it to take off, barking joyfully, after a butterfly or a falling leaf. The Afghan needs to know who's boss or this king of dogs will certainly rule. This intelligent, sensitive dog must, however, be trained kindly.

These pages: **The long, silky coat of the Afghan comes in a variety of colors and requires frequent brushing. This ancient breed has a dignified and aloof appearance.**

AIREDALE TERRIER

The largest of the terriers, the Airedale is known as the king of terriers. The Airedale was created in the middle of the last century to deal with the otters which were competing with the fishermen for the fish in the River Aire in Yorkshire. The Airedale has a natural affinity for water and enjoys splashing around in the marshes, which are home to the otter.

The Airedale's ancestors were the English Black and Tan Terrier (a breed which is now extinct) and the Otterhound. From the former, the breed inherited keen hearing and eyesight, and from the latter its excellent sense of smell, strength and powerful swimming stroke.

The Airedale Terrier is very versatile. In addition to otters, it has been used to track larger game, such as deer, wild boar and bear, and it is a swift and sure destroyer of small predators. During the First World War, the Airedale served its country as a battlefield messenger and sentry for the US Army. It has also worked as a police dog, putting some teeth into the law. Today the Airedale is primarily a faithful pet and protector of the home and family.

Although the Airedale is not quarrelsome, the breed has never been known to walk away from a fight. Still, the Airedale remains a puppy at heart, is lively and playful, and may track an imaginary critter under a dining room chair. This dog probably gets its sweet disposition from the lovable Otterhound.

The Airedale looks like a giant, rough terrier. Its coat, which needs daily brushing and regular stripping and trimming, is dark tan with black or dark grizzle and consists of a dense undercoat covered with a hard, wiry top coat. The head is long and flat, with small, alert dark eyes, folded ears and a black nose. The body is short, with well-sprung ribs and muscular loins. The Airedale is leggy, standing between 22 and 24 inches tall at the shoulder, with plenty of muscle and bone, and carries its tail, docked to a fair length, gaily.

After being shown at the Airedale Agricultural Society's 1879 show in Yorkshire, England, the Airedale became more well known. It arrived in the United States at the turn of the century and soon became top dog. In the 1920s, calling a man a 'regular Airedale' marked him as a ladies' man and a dandy.

Since then the breed has had its ups and downs in popularity, but recently has gained in favor, not just in Britain, but also in Germany, Canada and the United States.

These pages: **Though once a working terrier, the Airedale's friendly and alert personality makes it a favorite pet.**

AKITA

The Japanese Akita, like the Japanese Bobtail, has been designated a national monument. While the tricolored, twisted-tailed cat, with paw raised in greeting, symbolizes good luck, the powerful, good-natured dog, with broad head, alert ears and large, curled tail is a symbol of good health. A small statue of an Akita, signifying health, happiness and a long life, is often presented to the parents of a newborn baby. Similarly, sending one of these figurines to a sick person conveys the message: 'Get well soon!'

Japanese mothers have left their children in the care of the family Akita for generations, for the Akita is very affectionate and enjoys human companionship, and if a person or animal threatens the family, the Akita will rush to its defense.

The Akita is mentioned in historical documents of the seventeenth century, when the breed was being perfected through selective breeding. Yet it dates back beyond that time, because an Akita's image has been found carved on the tombs of the early Japanese people.

In ancient times the Akita was used for hunting bear, deer and wild boar in the rugged mountain region of Northern Japan, called Akita. A pair of Akitas, a male and a female, working as a team, would hold the Yezo, a huge, ferocious bear, at bay until the hunter arrived with spear or bow and arrow. *Matagi* means 'esteemed hunter' and only those men of a village with the best hunting skills bore this designation. The Akita was known as *Matagiinu*, 'esteemed dog hunter.'

Because the Akita has a soft mouth, it was also used to retrieve waterfowl felled by the hunter's arrow and, being an excellent swimmer, it was employed to force fish into the fisherman's nets. The Akita's double coat keeps it from freezing in the wintertime. This versatile, intelligent, courageous dog will do anything its master asks him to do.

Fidelity is another characteristic of the Akita. In the first quarter of the twentieth century Dr Eisaburo Ueno, a professor at Tokyo University, had an Akita named *Hachiko* that accompanied him daily to the train station to see him off. The dog returned to the station each afternoon to welcome his master back. Then one day in May 1925, Professor Ueno died at the university, and the faithful *Hachiko* waited in vain at the station until midnight. For nine years after that *Hachiko* went to the station every day, looking for his beloved master, and stayed till midnight. Only the dog's death in March 1934, ended his nightly vigil. A statue of *Hachiko* was erected at Tokyo's Shibuya railroad station and each year there is a solemn ceremony at the station to commemorate the loyalty and devotion of the professor's pet.

Helen Keller is said to have brought the first Akitas into the United States, having been given her first Akita upon visiting the Prefecture of Akita in 1937. After World War II, American servicemen, impressed with the breed's intelligence and ability to adapt to varying situations, brought them home with them to the US.

Today the Akita is often used as a police and guard dog, and is prized as a house pet. The breed was admitted to registration in the American Kennel Club Stud Book in October 1972, and soon after to regular show classification in the Working Group at American Kennel Club shows.

Below: **A playful Akita puppy. The Akita's coat comes in many colors, and some Akitas, like the one** *at right,* **have a mask or blaze.**

ALASKAN MALAMUTE

The Alaskan Malamute is the native Alaskan Arctic breed. It is related to the Samoyed of Russia, the Siberian Husky and the Eskimo dogs of Greenland and Labrador, as well as other Spitz dogs, such as the Akita of Japan. It has been suggested that the Alaskan natives may have been pulled into Alaska on dog sleds during the Glacier Age, when the land is thought to have connected Asia and Alaska, Greenland and Labrador.

This famous sled dog, known through the tales of Jack London and Rudyard Kipling, was named after the native Indian tribe called Mahlemuts that settled in Alaska in the far distant past. The Mahlemuts, now spelled Malamutes, worked hard, were skilled in hunting and fishing, built perfect sleds, and had beautiful and strong dogs. The Malamutes are never mentioned without reference to their dogs.

The Mahlemuts, according to one early traveler, 'though uncivilized . . . realized that it is important to have fine animals to pull sledges; that without them, means of travel in this sort of country would be impossible at times.' Another visitor noted: 'These dogs . . . traveled . . . hundreds of miles and [were] better cared for by their drivers than is the usual lot of Arctic dogs . . . [they] were affectionate and seemed tireless . . . .' A Russian admitted the 'Mahlemut dogs and sledges are better than those of the Russians for interior travel.'

Although the Alaskan Malamute is wolflike in appearance, it is not wolfish in personality, but is an affectionate, sociable, intelligent, playful companion. The Malamute is also faithful, docile, devoted, very clean and not given to unnecessary barking. This dignified dog, weighing between 75 and 85 pounds, is heavily boned and powerfully built, with a deep chest and strong, compact body. It has a double coat, usually gray or black and white, to protect it against the fierce Alaskan weather. The head is broad and strong with dark eyes. (Blue eyes are a disqualifying fault.) The feet are made for walking over the snow, large with thick, tough pads, and fur between the toes. The tail is carried over the body and resembles a waving plume.

The Alaskan Malamute has been recognized by the American Kennel Club since 1935.

These pages: **The Malamute moves with a proud carriage, head erect and eyes alert. They are affectionate dogs and make friends easily.**

AMERICAN FOXHOUND

The American Foxhound's bark is so melodious it has been incorporated into popular songs. It doubtless inherited its good voice from its French Foxhound ancestors, which were said to sing 'like the bells of Moscow.'

According to authorities, it was De Soto who brought the first hounds to America to seek out Indians, and not foxes and hares. Then, in 1650, Robert Drooke settled in Maryland and brought his English Foxhounds with him. These formed the foundation stock of several important American Foxhound strains and remained in the family for 300 years. George Washington bought some English hounds in 1770 and was given some French hounds by Lafayette in 1785. He crossed the two varieties and produced the American Foxhound.

In the early nineteenth century some of the best English hounds were imported and more French hounds were brought over, as well as Irish hounds. The latter were the fountainhead of the Birdsong and Trigg families. Other famous American strains are the Walker, Kedbone, and Gossett.

Influenced, perhaps, by the musical tones coming from the hounds, hardriding Marylanders and Virginians, upon catching sight of the fox, would commence an exuberant falsetto yipping. This spontaneous, excited chorus may, in turn, have inspired the scary rebel yells of the Confederate soldiers.

Guided by the hounds' distant chorusing, American huntsmen participate in the pastime of hilltopping, whereby, around a campfire, each hunter listens for his own hounds 'speaking to the line' as they pursue their quarry through the night. These hunts end when the fox finds his burrow. Afterward, if not summoned to return by horns, the hounds go home of their own accord, owing to an inbred homing instinct.

Horsemen in formal attire follow the pack in more than 100 traditional hunts each year on the East and West Coasts of the United States. They enjoy a good gallop even if the bait is not a real fox but only a scented lure. And the echoing melody of the foxhounds remains in the memory of those who hear it.

The American Foxhound is slightly leggier and lighter than its English cousin, and has the speed and stamina to give the fox a race it won't forget. The Foxhound has so much energy he can run around a square-mile farm from sunup till late night and return home still spirited and ready to run some more.

While similar to the English Foxhound, the American Foxhound also has a better sense of smell and a longer head and ears. Both weigh 65 to 70 pounds, and their short-haired coats come in all colors. The American Foxhound has large, wide-set eyes, which are either brown or hazel, with a gentle, imploring expression. When not hunting, this dog makes a sweet and affectionate companion.

Below: **The long legs on the American Foxhound give it the speed it needs for pursuing a fox.** *Right:* **The breed standard calls for wide-set eyes and long ears, set low and held close to the head.**

AMERICAN STAFFORDSHIRE TERRIER

The Staffordshire Bull Terrier arrived in America in 1870. To begin with, it was called the American Bull Terrier, the Yankee Terrier, the Pit Bull Dog, or simply the Pit Dog.

The breed was accepted for registration in the American Kennel Club Stud Book as the Staffordshire Terrier in 1936, changed in 1972 to the American Staffordshire Terrier. Breeders in America, having developed a dog some 10 pounds heavier than the English variety, wanted to distinguish this American dog from his English ancestor.

Originally bred as a fighting dog until dog fighting was banned, now the American Staffordshire Terrier is bred for strength, affection, intelligence, watchfulness and courage. It is a good watch dog and is able to distinguish between strangers with good intentions and those with bad intentions.

Generally, the breed resembles the Staffordshire Terrier. Its ears may be cropped or uncropped, any color coat is permissible, and its nose should be black, never pink.

AMERICAN WATER SPANIEL

With its tail as a rudder, the American Water Spaniel swims like a seal and few wounded fowl get away. The American Water Spaniel is also an all-around hunting dog with an excellent nose and attitude. It springs the game, patiently watches the hunter drop four or five birds — pheasant, duck, grouse or quail — and then joyfully goes to work. Whatever the terrain — bushy, rough ground, or wooded — this dog's enthusiasm and eagerness to please are always present as it goes to fetch the birds.

Just where this wondrous water spaniel, which is principally known in the Midwest, originated is something of a mystery. In appearance it looks like a cross between an Irish Water Spaniel and the Curly-Coated Retriever, along with the latter's ancestor, the old English Water Spaniel. It is known as the Boykin Spaniel in some parts of the country, after Whit Boykin, an early breeder in South Carolina.

Because this breed's admirers seemingly feared introduction to the show ring might damage its hunting ability, the American Water Spaniel was recognized as a breed by the American Kennel Club only in 1940, even though it was known in the United States for many years. Those promoters of this breed learned that selective breeding and competition with dogs of equal stature enhance a dog's value even, if it has not been born with the best hunting ability.

The American Water Spaniel has a solid liver or dark chocolate coat, which is tightly curled and acts as a protective cover against weather, water or rough terrain. Of medium size, this dog weighs between 25 and 45 pounds. Its head is of moderate length, with a rather broad skull and a slight stop. The ears are pendulous and covered with curls and the eyes are hazel, brown or of a dark color which harmonizes with the coat. They are set well apart and have an awake, intelligent expression. The tail is slightly curved and feathered. This sturdily constructed, symmetrical animal makes a capable watchdog and a fine family pet.

Right: **The American Staffordshire Terrier is a strong, muscular dog. Although the dog has a stocky build, it is agile and graceful. Like its British cousin — the Staffordshire Bull Terrier — it is well known for its courage.**

AUSTRALIAN CATTLE DOG

The Australian Cattle Dog was created to herd half-wild cattle over long distances. As Australian settlers began spreading outside the Sydney area, in 1813, vast grazing lands were opened up and cattle allowed to roam freely. Unlike the quiet and controlled cattle that lived on smaller ranches around Sydney, these animals were semiwild and hard to control.

A black, bobtailed dog, known as the Smithfield, was the most popular dog used by the early cattle owners and drovers, but, like other herding dogs then in use, the Smithfield found the new road to market too long and too rough. In addition, this dog's natural inclination was to bark a lot and head the cattle, which worked well with the tamer town variety, but only made the plains cattle stampede and run in all directions.

Around 1830 cattle ranchers called for a dog with more stamina that would work quietly and yet effectively to get the unruly animals to the Sydney saleyards. A stockman by the name of Timmins answered the call by crossing a Smithfield with a dingo, which resulted in red, bobtailed dogs, named Timmins Biters. These dogs were silent, but overly fierce in snapping at the cattle's heels and difficult to keep in check. They were used for awhile, but gradually died out. In 1840, Thomas Hall, a property owner, imported a pair of smooth-haired Highland Collies from Scotland, which had sufficient energy for the long trip to market, but which also barked and headed. He crossed their offspring with the dingo—and Hall's Heelers were born. They were red or blue merle, most had upright ears, and dingo-shaped heads and bodies. Because these silent herders worked better than any that had gone before them, they were much in demand.

George Elliott, in Queensland, also crossed blue merle Collies with dingoes and developed an excellent strain. Two brothers, Jack and Harry Bagust, in Sydney, bought puppies from George Elliott and arranged a match between a female and a Dalmatian, upon which the merle became a red or blue speckle. The Bagusts' aim—to produce a dog which would naturally love horses and be unwaveringly faithful to his master—was achieved, but some of the herding ability was lost. The brothers, noticing how well the Black and Tan Kelpie herded sheep, decided to mate their speckled dogs with some

of them. They were pleased with the product, which resembled the dingo, but was heavier set. There were blue dogs with black patches around brown eyes, a small white patch on the forehead and tan markings on the head, chest, and legs, and red dogs with dark red markings and an over-all red speckle. These dogs became the forebears of the modern Australian Cattle Dog, and were known as Blue Heelers, for the blue variety was more popular. In Queensland they were dubbed Queensland Heelers or Queensland Blue Heelers.

Robert Koleski began breeding these dogs in 1893 and was showing them in 1897. By 1902 he had a standard for the Cattle Dog as well as for the Kelpie and the Barb. Believing the native dog of Australia to be best suited to cope with conditions in his homeland, he based the Cattle Dog largely on the dingo. The Australian Heeler, later the Australian Cattle Dog, was approved by the Cattle and Sheep Dog Club of Australia and the original Kennel Club in 1903. The breed was accepted for registration by the American Kennel Club in 1980 after a time in the Miscellaneous breed category.

At last the Australian cattle owners had their ideal dog—one with staying power, reliability, intelligence, and a speckled coat which camouflages it as it goes quietly about its herding duties, nipping at the cows' heels.

AUSTRALIAN KELPIE

A pair of smooth-coated Collies were brought out from Scotland in 1870, and mated before the ship docked. Their puppies were born in Australia and started the Kelpie breed in that country. The dingo entered the picture soon after, adding its characteristics to the breed.

The Australian Kelpie weighs about 30 pounds, is well muscled and comes in a variety of colors, including red, red and tan, fawn, chocolate, blue black, and black and tan. Its eyes are dark, almond-shaped and very expressive.

This marvelous sheep dog works tirelessly and often without supervision. The Kelpie is very fast and ready to respond at once to any signal given by its master, even from a great distance. It's said the Kelpie does the work of six men on grazing land so sparse it takes up to 10 acres to feed one sheep. The Australian Kelpie is the most common working sheep dog in Australia and New Zealand today. Although handicapped with a leg injury, *Coil*, a champion Kelpie, won two Australian national championships in 1898, which illustrates this breed's vigor and determination.

Below: **When they reach adulthood, these Australian Kelpies will be tireless workers.** *Right:* **Kelpies make good pets, too.**

AUSTRALIAN TERRIER

The Australian Terrier was developed by Australians to hunt rodents and rabbits. Also a star snake killer, the Aussie bounds into the air and pounces on the reptile from the rear. Several terriers went into the making of the Australian Terrier, although there is some question as to exactly which ones. Most authorities agree the Aussie has Cairn, Dandie Dinmont, Irish Terrier, Black and Tan (now Manchester Terrier), Yorkshire and Sky blood coursing through his veins. The AKC welcomed this playful little pet into its registry in 1960.

With so many different ancestors, the Aussie has all the more possibility of having a unique personality. This terrier may be keenly alert or slightly spacey, daydreaming perhaps about a seasoned, buried bone, a successful rat kill or a recent play session with a ball. The Aussie makes a charming pet as well as a good guard dog. This dog has a happy disposition, is intelligent, affectionate, vivacious, hardy and courageous.

The Australian Terrier's double, waterproof coat, which comes in red, blue, silver grey and sandy, allows it to sleep indoors or out. Weighing nine to 11 pounds, this low-set, compact terrier has a toy dog appearance, which adds to its appeal. The head is long and flat, with a slight but definite stop, topped by little upright ears, and set off by small, alert, dark eyes. The Aussie wears its tail docked.

BASENJI

The Basenji is known as the barkless dog because, instead of a bark, it utters a sound somewhere between a chortle and a yodel. The Basenji usually gives voice when he is contented, which is a good bit of the time, for this dog has a happy character, and accompanies this with glad tail-wagging. The smallest event will cause the Basenji to prick up its ears and fine and profuse wrinkles to appear on its forehead, giving it a characteristic and appealing surprised look.

The Basenji loves children and never tires of playing. To get people's attention, the Basenji has an intriguing way of bringing one front paw behind its ear, then down over its nose, and repeating this motion until getting a response. When the Basenji has worn out its owner, it will lie down devotedly at his feet. The Basenji has a habit of washing itself with its paw, like a cat, and keeps its short, silky hair immaculately clean. A red dog's coat gleams like polished copper in the sun.

This fine-boned, aristocratic-looking, little hound's gait resembles the trot of a racehorse. In its native Congo, it sometimes leaps high to see over the tall elephant grass and is called the 'jumping-up-and-down dog.' The Basenji is also known by many other names: Zande Dog, Belgian Congo Dog, Congo Bush Dog, Bongo Terrier, Congo Terrier, and Nyam-Nyam Terrier. Basenji is derived from an African word meaning 'bush thing.'

The Basenji is about the size of a Fox Terrier, weighing between 22 and 24 pounds. This breed has far-seeing, dark hazel, diamond-shaped eyes and a tightly-curled tail, carried to either side. Its coat is chestnut red, black, or black and tan, all with white feet, chest, and tail tip. Owing to its beauty, graceful carriage, and intelligence, the Basenji has often been compared to a little deer.

One of the most ancient of breeds, the Basenji originated in Egypt over 5000 years ago, and the first specimens were brought as presents to the Pharaohs. Then, when Egyptian civilization declined and fell, the companion of Egypt's nobles dropped from sight. Yet the dog was still valued in Central Africa for his speed, hunting ability, intelligence, and sometimes for its silence.

Tribal hunters often hang a bell around his neck to create a din, start game in the bush, and drive it into nets. He is also used for pointing, retrieving, and hunting for wounded quarry, when its silence is an important asset. Though gentle as a kitten, this brave little dog has been known to hunt the vicious, long-toothed reed rat, which weighs almost as much as it does, between 12 and 20 pounds.

An English explorer rediscovered the Basenji in the Congo, in 1895, and brought a few dogs back to England. Unfortunately, they all died of distemper before he could start a dynasty. This exotic canine was not heard from again outside of Africa until 1937 when more specimens arrived in England and survived. A pair was also brought to America at this time and a litter was born; sadly, all died except the older male dog, *Bois*. In 1941, *Bois* was joined by a young female, named *Congo*, and they produced the first litter of Basenji puppies to survive to adulthood in America. The Basenji Club of America was formed in 1942 and this unique and charming little dog was accepted for registration by the AKC in 1943.

BASSET HOUND

The Basset Hound is identified with Hush Puppy shoes and was probably selected to represent that brand because it looks the way the shoes are supposed to feel — comfortable, soft and kind (to tired feet).

Before the Basset became a symbol for shoes, this sturdy little hound with the dark, soulful eyes bravely tracked a variety of game,

continued on page 30

These pages: The Basset Hound has a mild and devoted personality and is never sharp or timid.

Above: The Basset's short legs and heavy body make it ideally suited to follow a trail over rough and difficult terrain.

continued from page 26

such as deer, wolf, boar, fox and badger, in northern Europe's forests. French noblemen in sixteenth century France went badger hunting with Bassets in high style. According to a contemporary writer, absolute necessities were at least a dozen well-trained Bassets, wearing thick collars with bells on them; carpets on which to recline and listen to the sweet voices of the hounds as they pursued their prey underground; and a dozen strong men to dig down and pull the badger from his barrow. In the Middle Ages in France several varieties of low-slung dogs emerged from local strains of hounds and in time became known as the short-haired Basset Ardennais, Artésien Normand, d'Artois and Bleu de Gascogne and the wire-haired Basset Fauve de Bretagne and Griffon Vendéen. Some had straight legs, others crooked. The friars of the French Abbey of St Hubert are credited with creating the lower-set, slower-moving hounds, which could be followed on foot. Their name, 'Basset,' comes from the French adjective *bas* meaning 'low' or 'short.'

Shakespeare poetically and yet realistically described the Basset Hound in *A Midsummer Night's Dream*: 'Their heads are hung with ears that sweep away the morning dew; crook-knee'd, and dew-lapp'd like Thessalian bulls; slow in pursuit but match'd in mouth like bells . . . '

Although Englishmen had heard about the Basset Hound, few had seen one prior to 1863, when they were exhibited at the first dog show held in Paris and captured the public's fancy. Twelve years later, at a dog show in Britain, the Basset was discovered by British royalty. King Edward VII and Queen Alexandra became Basset fanciers. Sir Edward Millais added the Bloodhound strain to his Basset stock, which consisted primarily of the Basset-Artésien Normand. This changed somewhat the appearance of the dog, giving it a head resembling the Bloodhound and slack skin, and improved its scenting ability.

In the United States, George Washington was made a gift of Basset Hounds by Lafayette after the American Revolution, and subsequently more of the velvet-eared hounds were imported from Britain by Basset enthusiasts. The excellent English import *Nemours* was presented to the American public at the Westminster Kennel Club show in 1884, and completed his championship at Boston in 1886. Bassets were first accepted for registration by the AKC in 1885.

Time magazine drew more attention to the breed when a Basset puppy was on the cover of the 27 February 1928 issue, and the accompanying story was all about the fifty-second annual Westminster Kennel Club Dog Show at Madison Square as seen through the puppy's eyes. By the 1950s in England, the cartoon strip *Fred Basset* had humanized the mild-natured, droll-faced hound by making him stand for Everyman.

Although at present the Basset is mainly a family pet, it retains strong hound instincts and may wander if the gate is left open. The Basset has a mind of its own and requires discipline. Because it has lots of energy, this dog needs fields in which to romp or to go for long walks. Some hunters still take him rabbit hunting.

BEAGLE

There is some question as to where this smallest of the English hounds got its name. One theory is that Beagle comes from the Celtic *beag*, meaning small. Another is that it derives from medieval French *Begle*, shortened from *bégueule*, signifying 'one who whines insistently.'

When one hears the word *Beagle*, most people think of Snoopy, probably the most popular Beagle of all. Presented to the public in 1950 by Charles M Schultz, Snoopy is a white-coated Beagle with black ears, coloring which would instantly disqualify him at a dog show. He is known for his philosophic musings and comments as pointed as his nose. He is also famous for his journeys in search of his origins.

The latter is fitting because the beginnings of the Beagle are shrouded in mist. Some experts claim he originated in Greece, was employed in France as a hare hunter, arrived in England with

Right: **Though smaller in size, the Beagle resembles the Foxhound in appearance.**

William the Conqueror in 1066, and was probably developed in Elizabethan times by crossing ancient English hounds with the Harrier. Others hold there were packs of hounds in England before the time of the Romans, and state that Pwyll, Prince of Wales, a contemporary of King Arthur, kept a pack of white hounds of superior quality. They further assert that this hound was the forefather of all sporting dogs which rely on their noses.

In the sixteenth century, during the developmental period of the Beagle, two sizes of dogs came into being: those under 12 inches at the withers and those over 12 inches at the withers. Queen Elizabeth I especially liked the very small beagles, which had a bell-like bark, and were known as pocket Beagles because they were small enough to fit into the pocket of a hunting coat. Because Queen Bess kept a pack of these singing Beagles, they were also called Elizabeth Beagles. Unfortunately, these smaller dogs are now extinct. The larger Beagles were referred to as vaches, or Buck Hounds, and were used to hunt deer while the smaller hounds were used for hares.

In the mid nineteenth century, Parson Honeywood of Essex hunted with such a fine pack that a leading artist did an engraving of *The Merry Beaglers*, attracting the attention of sportsmen and bringing great popularity to the hound and the sport. Honeywood's hounds resembled English foxhounds in miniature.

It's not clear when Beagles first arrived in the United States, but it is known they existed in the Southern States prior to 1870, when they were mostly white with few dark markings, and looked more like Bassets, Dachshunds—or even Snoopy. The National Beagle Club, founded in 1888, introduced New Englanders to a new diversion: Beagle Field Trials. In these tournaments, Beagles compete in pairs in a rabbit patch, eagerly working together to trace the rabbit and singing a melodious duet. Judges watch for technique and penalize hounds that putter at a cold trail. They need not kill the rabbit to win the prize.

Beagles are so tractable, they easily learn to flush quail and other birds or to run a fox to earth. In Australia, Beagles join their tenor voices in song after medium-sized kangaroos, and some Beagles like to jump in the water and go fishing.

Although Beagles have been a joy to hunters for hundreds of years and are still used for hunting in many areas of the world, today they are more often kept as companion dogs, where they are content to track down only their owners' slippers.

Below: **Nowadays the Beagle is primarily a pet, but the breed still retains its hunting instincts.** *Right:* **An adorable Beagle puppy.**

BEARDED COLLIE

While the origin of the Bearded Collie is somewhat vague, it is now generally thought that it, like most shaggy-haired herding dogs, including the Old English Sheepdog, descends from the Hungarian Komondor of central Europe. It is a fact that two female and one male Magyar sheep dogs were brought to Scotland by Polish traders in 1414 and exchanged for a ram and a ewe. Originally known as the Hairy Mountain Dog, and later as the Highland Collie, the Mountain Collie, or the Hairy Mou'ed Collie, the Bearded Collie resembles the French Briard, the Hungarian Puli and Komondor, and the Italian Bergamasco Sheepdog in body structure and coat type.

Although there are few early records on this friendly, shaggy dog, we first catch sight of one in a 1771 Gainsborough portrait of the Duke of Buccleigh and in a 1772 Reynolds portrait of the painter's wife and daughter. The existence of the breed was firmly established in the early nineteenth century with Reinagle's portrait, entitled *Sheepdog*, which appeared in Taplin's 1803 Sportsman's Cabinet, and with a detailed description of the Bearded Collie in the 1818 edition of the *Livestock Journal*.

At the end of the Victorian era, Beardies continued to be popular as sheepherding and show dogs. Because there was no breed club,

however, there was no official standard, and each judge based his decision on his own idea of the dog. By the 1930s, Bearded Collies were no longer being bred for show purposes, and 10 years later the breed was almost extinct. Only shepherds still had Beardies, for they knew the value of these loyal sheep dogs that put in a day's work in the worst weather.

Mrs GO Willison, in 1944, acquired an unregistered female Beardie puppy and bought a male from his owners at the beach and began a breeding program for show purposes, resurrecting the breed form this one breeding pair. She was active in the establishment of the Bearded Collie Club in Britain in 1955, and was at least partially responsible for the increasing popularity of the breed.

Bearded Collies made their debut in America in the late 1950s, and the Bearded Collie Club of America was founded in 1969. They were shown in the Miscellaneous class at first, but were moved to the Working Group in 1977, and finally to the Herding Group in 1983.

The Bearded Collie is medium sized; comes in black, blue, shades of grey, fawn and sandy; and has large, expressive, gentle, loving eyes. This excellent herder lifts its feet only enough to clear the ground, thus gliding along, making the sharp turns and the quick stops required of the sheep dog. The Bearded Collie has a second use as a drover. Working with little direction, the Beardie is very successful at moving cattle.

Below: **A Bearded Collie and his best friend.** *Right:* **The Beardie is obviously a cousin of the Old English Sheepdog** *(see page 136).*

BEDLINGTON TERRIER

The Bedlington looks like a little lamb, and one almost expects it to say ''baa' instead of ''bow wow,' but exteriors can be deceiving, and within this fragile appearing body there beats a lionlike heart. This courageous dog has a mild and gentle expression, but when aroused it is particularly alert and full of immense energy. Noted for its endurance, the Bedlington can gallop at great speeds, as its body outline shows. The Bedlington has a unique lightness of movement, and even at a slow pace, it has a springy step.

The Bedlington Terrier was much prized by the coal miners of the shire of Bedlington, in the County of Northumberland, England, for its courage and versatility. After a day spent down in the mines, the miners took great pleasure in watching this small, woolly, blue dog race, for it ran like a blue streak. When it rained, a barn or a shed could always be found for a dog fight or a rat-killing contest. The Bedlington was also good at hunting various forms of vermin, including rats, mice, rabbits, badgers and otters, and popular as a poacher's dog, earning him the nickname 'Gypsy Dog.'

While the exact origin of the Bedlington is a mystery, it is certain the Dandie Dinmont Terrier is one of his ancestors, and bequeathed him his vermin-killing skill, and the Whippet contributed a more svelte form, longer legs and swiftness of movement. Although the Bedlington was developed around 1825 by English miners who wanted a dog that would exterminate the rats and mice in the mines, the breed was not recognized by the AKC until rather late in the twentieth century. Today the Bedlington is a loyal and affectionate companion and guard dog.

The Bedlington Terrier can be colored blue, sandy, liver, blue and tan, sandy and tan or liver and tan. The preferred height is 15.5 to 16.5 inches at the withers and the weight should be between 17 and 23 pounds. With his distinctive pearshaped head, small deep-set eyes, fringed ears, roached back, curly coat — trimmed somewhat like a poodle's — and long, slender tail, the Bedlington would never be mistaken for any other breed.

BELGIAN MALINOIS

The Belgian Malinois is one of the four Belgian sheep dogs that evolved from a variety of ancient herding dogs. Examples of these herding dogs appear in fifteenth century drawings alongside the Dukes of Bourgogne and Hapsburg. For a long time, these herding cousins guarded the flocks in the Belgian and European countrysides. Then, late in the nineteenth century, as more and more open land was fenced in and crisscrossed by railways and roads, they lost their jobs.

Belgian dog fanciers, afraid these dogs might disappear altogether, combined their efforts to preserve the breed. They agreed on everything but the kind of coat and color. Hence the four varieties: the short-haired Malinois, from the city of Malines; the long-haired Groenendael and Tervuren; and the wire-haired Laekenois. All these dogs are registered in Belgium and France as the *Chien de Berger Belge*.

Charlot, born in 1891, was one of the first short-coated Belgian shepherds, and served as a model of the Belgian Malinois for the Belgian artist A Clary. Known for its excellent herding ability, and having won more prizes in competition than the other three types, the Malinois has historically been the favorite sheeperder in Belgium. The first short-haired Belgian sheep dogs registered with the American Kennel Club in 1911 were *Belgian Blackie* and *Belgian Mouche*.

With its easy-care coat, elegant appearance, intelligence and trainability, the Malinois is popular for hunting, herding, sledding, tracking and simply as a family pet. The breed resembles the German Shepherd, but is smaller — males measuring 24 to 26 inches in height at the withers, and females 22 to 24 inches. Its distinctive black mask and ears contrast nicely with the rich fawn to mahogany coloring on the rest of its body. The Malinois has a light and easy gait and never seems to tire.

BELGIAN SHEPHERD DOG (GROENENDAEL)

The discovery of a single black female puppy in a litter of Belgian herding dogs, in the late nineteenth century, set Nicolas Rose, a restaurateur in the village of Groenendael, on a quest to find a similar black male with which to mate her and create a new breed, the Belgian Shepherd Dog, or Groenendael. Because black dogs were scarce then, Monsieur Rose searched for nearly a year before he found an appropriate mate, and began a breeding program.

Picard d'Uccle and *Petite* were the proud parents of *Pitt, Baronne* and *Duc de Groenendael*, and they, along with their offspring formed the foundation stock of the Belgian Shepherd Dog. At the dog show where the breed made its debut, in 1898, these handsome ebony dogs, with the slightly elongated heads and plumed tails, caught the public's fancy.

Although the Groenendael was known as a sheep dog, people quickly became aware of its versatility, owing to its keen intelligence and trainability. During the early twentieth century, the Groenendael became a Parisian and a New York police dog and was employed as a border patrol dog in Belgium, helping customs authorities catch smugglers. At the same time, Belgian Sheep Dogs began winning prizes at European working trials, and one dog *Jules du Moulin*, became an international champion many times over.

During the First World War, Belgian Shepherds served as message carriers and red cross aides on the battlefield. They searched for and found wounded soldiers and carried messages through the crossfire, and even pulled machine guns. Again, in the Second World War, these brave dogs worked for the military, guarding military posts. On the home front, when used as guard dogs in bars, these beautiful black animals sit quietly and never bother the customers; but once the place has closed for the night an intruder is in danger of a vicious attack.

While going about its herding duties on western ranches in the United States, the Belgian Sheepdog, unlike the German Shepherd, does not risk being mistaken for a coyote or a prairie wolf and shot, for its black coloring distinguishes it from those animals. Belgian Shepherds are capable of many different feats — tracking, guarding, herding, guiding, pulling sleds — but they are probably most valuable as loyal and devoted companions. And with their sleek black coats and elegant carriage, they are a joy to behold.

By a 1959 AKC ruling, only a Groenendael can be registered as a Belgian Sheepdog, and it must have three generations of Groenendael ancestors.

BELGIAN TERVUEREN

In November 1891 shepherd dogs of all colors, coats, and sizes were gathered together at the Brussels Veterinary University on the outskirts of Belgium. Professor Adolphe Reul, a veterinarian, and a group of judges examined over a hundred dogs and concluded that all were physically alike — they were square, medium-sized sheepdogs, with erect ears, dark brown eyes, finely chiselled heads, long tails, and brisk and even movements, but their coats had different hair lengths, colors and textures.

Professor Reul's notes on the various dogs led to the first written standard, in 1893, and recognition by the Société Royale Saint-Hubert in 1901. Four types of Belgian sheepherding dogs were eventually distinguished: Groenendael, with long, straight, black fur; Tervueren, with long, straight fur of any color but black and black mask and ears, and sometimes with black overlay; Malinois, with short red or fawn coat and black overlay and black mask and ears; and Laekenois, with a rough, dry, untidy looking reddish fawn coat.

A Monsieur Corbeel, from the village of Tervueren, developed the Belgian Tervueren. He bred *Tom* and *Poes*, a fawn-colored couple, whose offspring included fawn-colored *Miss*. She, then, was mated

Right: The Belgian Tervueren is intelligent, courageous, alert and devoted to its master.

with the black *Duc de Groenendael*, and produced *Milsart*, the famous fawn dog, which, in 1907, became the first Tervueren champion.

Yet it was not until after World War II that people began to take notice of the Tervueren. As sometimes happens, a Tervueren was born in a Groenendael litter; *Willy de la Garde Noire* was pale fawn in color and of perfect conformation. He won numerous firsts in Belgium and France during the 1950s, and was such a successful producer that he was responsible for the spread of the Tervueren, especially in France, but also in the rest of Europe and the United States.

The Belgian Tervueren has continued to work as a sheepherder, but has expanded his capabilities; it is also used as a therapy dog and companion to the disabled, search and rescue dog (including avalanche rescue work), sentry and courier in wartime and as a tracker. All of the Belgian shepherds are intelligent, courageous, easily trained, affectionate and devoted to their owners. The rare Laekenois is not recognized in the United States.

BERNESE MOUNTAIN DOG

Considered 'the most beautiful dog in the world' by at least one canine authority, the Bernese Mountain Dog is one of four Swiss Mountain Dogs. The others are the Great Swiss Sennenhund, the Appenzell Sennenhund and the Entlebuch Sennenhund. They are named after the regions in which they were found, and all are believed to have descended from big Molossian- or Mastiff-like dogs brought into ancient Helvetia by Roman legions at the time of the Roman conquests twenty centuries ago. These large dogs were used to herd their cattle and guard their military positions and trading posts. Wearing spiked collars, they may also have gone forth to battle with their masters. Images of dogs resembling the present-day mountain dogs have been found on clay objects from the time of the

Below: **A Belgian Tervueren puppy.** *Right:* **The Bernese Mountain Dog has a soft, silky, long and slightly wavy coat.**

Roman invasions. The four dogs are known in Switzerland as Sennenhunde, which means 'cheesemaker's dogs,' because they were used to pull dairymen's carts.

Once common in the Swiss mountains, the Bernese — which takes its name from the Canton of Bern — lost ground in about 1840 to its cousin, the Saint Bernard, whose early history is similar, and other dogs and, in fact, almost died out. The breed was revived and saved by two Swiss dog fanciers, one of whom, Franz Schertenlieb, in 1892, found the best remaining specimens around the village of Durrbach and, with Professor Albert Heim, started a breeding program. Hence, the dog is often called the 'Durrbachler' This beautiful, intelligent, loyal, affectionate and good-natured dog was recognized by the British and American Kennel Clubs in the 1930s.

The compact body, broad chest, muscular forelegs and well-developed thighs mark the Bernese as born to harness. This dog is about the size of a Collie, with a sleek, long jet black coat, usually blazed with white on the foreface, chest, feet and tail tip, highlighted with russet brown or deep tan markings over the eyes and on the chest and feet.

BICHON FRISÉ

This jaunty little dog with the corkscrew curls and happy disposition is a descendant of the Barbet, a water spaniel, from which the name Barbichon, later shortened to Bichon, meaning lap dog, comes. Four categories of Bichons (the Bichon Maltese, the Bichon Bolognais, the Bichon Havanais and the Bichon Teneriffe) originated in the Mediterranean area, and were probably introduced by sailors to the Canary Islands before the fourteenth century. It was at this time that 'Teneriffe' was added to the small, white dog's name, to add exotic sizzle and increase its market value.

continued on page 44

Below: **A handsome Bernese Mountain Dog.** *Right:* **Though small in size, the Bichon Frisé is a hardy, fun loving dog.**

Above: **A Bichon Frisé family. These cuddly dogs make wonderful companions and house pets.**

continued from page 40

Italian sailors are credited with bringing the attractive and friendly Bichon Teneriffe back to Europe, where the breed was much admired by Italian nobility. It became a pampered and perfumed darling at European courts during the Renaissance, particularly in Spain under Philip II, where the dog was captured on canvas by Goya, in Russia under Catherine the Great, and in France under Francis I and Henry III. Then, after becoming a favorite again at the Court of Napoleon III, the wheel of fortune turned, and the Bichon Frisé became a guide dog to the blind and a street and circus dog, accompanying organ grinders and performing in fairs and circuses.

At the end of World War I in France, four fanciers of the breed worked at perfecting the lines of the dog, and by 1933 the official standard of the breed, a joint Franco-Belgian effort, was adopted by the Société Centrale Canine of France. In 1934 the French Kennel Club admitted the Bichon Frisé to its stud book and the International Canine Federation recognized the dog 'as a French-Belgian breed having the right to registration in the Book of Origins from all countries.' Madame Nizet de Leemans, president of the International Canine Federation suggested a name which truly represents the dog's characteristics — Bichon Frisé, curly-haired lap dog. Monsieur and Madame François Picault moved to the United States in 1956 and started raising Bichon Frisés. Two other breeders began breeding programs, and the merry little powder puff of a dog was launched in the US. The breed was admitted to regular show classification in the Non-Sporting Group at AKC shows in 1973.

Regular grooming and trimming are required to keep the Bichon Frisé looking its best. With its fluffy, white coat, appealing brown eyes, pleasing personality and lively carriage, it is easy to see why the Bichon Frisé has never totally exited the scene and is once again gaining in popularity.

These pages: Since its acceptance by the American Kennel Club in the early 1970s, the Bichon Frisé has become a popular show dog.

BLACK & TAN COONHOUND

The hunt starts at night with the release of the hounds into the woods, upon which the hunters settle down in a lantern-lit circle to wait for the dogs to give voice. Noses to the leaf-strewn ground, the dogs sniff and pad their way into the trees. The hunters listen. Finally, they hear a mellow yelp from deep in the woods. The hunters get up, knowing the dogs have a trail. Hurrying after the hounds, their lanterns giant fireflies in the gloom, the men now and again pause and listen as the hounds change direction.

Then they hear excitement in the hounds' voices, because they have treed the raccoon and are 'barking up.' The hunters hearts beat faster as they hasten toward the scene. Upon arrival, they hang their lanterns in a wide circle around the tree with its little bandit quarry. They then beam their flashlights up between the branches and two beady eyes glare back in response. The dogs bark and jump at the tree, smelling the raccoon, but frustrated in their attempts to reach him. Eyeball to eyeball with the wily rascal, the hunt is at an end. Like his ancestor the Bloodhound, the Black and Tan Coonhound does not kill his prey.

In addition to the Bloodhound, the Black and Tan is descended from the Foxhound, via America's own Virginia Foxhound. The Black and Tan is as American as the ground on which it runs, although its first forefather was probably the Talbot hound, known in England during the reign of William I, Duke of Normandy, in the eleventh century.

The Black and Tan Coonhound is a working dog, able to withstand cold and wet winters and hot and humid summers, and famous for its far-reaching, deep voice. Its head is finely modeled, with a medium stop and pendent lips. The Black and tan has round, chestnut-colored eyes, long, hanging ears, a muscular neck, a straight back and forelegs, and well-boned and muscled hindquarters. A strong tail completes the dog. Its coat is black, trimmed with tan markings on the muzzle, limbs and chest. The Black and Tan weighs between 23 and 27 pounds. As a result of careful, selective breeding to standardize the Black and Tan, the breed became the first coonhound recognized by the American Kennel Club.

BLOODHOUND

In spite of its name and reputation, the Bloodhound is a gentle and affectionate dog. The name is probably derived from its ability to track animals, usually wounded and bleeding, but the Bloodhound is best known for tracking men, particularly criminals. Some Bloodhounds have been credited with following a trail thirty hours after it was made.

Appearances can be deceiving — the powerful Bloodhound (these pages) is gentle, extremely affectionate and shy.

The Bloodhound, according to some authorities, was first brought to England by William the Conqueror; however, another theory maintains the breed was brought by pilgrims from the Holy Land. At one time referred to as black St Hubert, there were also red and white dogs, and it is likely that the modern Bloodhound is a descendent of dogs of all three colors. Today the Bloodhound is tan with black markings, although deep tan all over, while rare, is acceptable. The Bloodhound stands 23 to 27 inches and weighs from 80 to 100 pounds. The skin on its large, domed head is loose and ample, forming deep folds and wrinkles. Its wrinkles, along with a long muzzle, droopy eyelids and long, low-hung ears, give the Bloodhound a serious and somber expression.

BORDER COLLIE

The Border Collie, one of the world's finest sheepdogs, is descended from dogs brought to Scotland by the Vikings in the eighth and ninth centuries. This dog will herd anything, and, in fact, its ancestors in Scandinavia herded reindeer. It has been said that the Border Collie hypnotizes cattle with its eyes. The original Scandinavian dogs were later crossed with the Valée Sheepdog and other collies of the lowland and border counties of England and Scotland. The breed is named after the English-Scottish border. The British Kennel Club approved a standard for the Border Collie in July 1976. The breed has not yet been recognized by the American Kennel Club, but in recent years this energetic popular breed has developed quite a following in the United States.

The Border Collie has won many sheep dog trials and obedience competitions. It also makes an excellent guide dog for the blind. This working dog has been exported to many countries of the world where sheep are raised, and is particularly popular in Australia. The Border Collies is about 21 inches tall, and a variety of colors is permissible. There are two coat types: one moderately long and the other short and smooth. It is a well-proportioned, graceful dog known for its intelligence, speed and stamina. Working from sunrise till sunset, the Border Collie makes a first-rate companion when the day is done.

BORDER TERRIER

This utilitarian dog was bred in the hilly border area between Scotland and England to help the farmers in their fight against the powerful and predatory foxes, which stole poultry and other small animals. The Border Terrier shares a common ancestor with the Lakeland, Bedlington, and Dandie Dinmont Terriers. The Redesdale, an all-white terrier, now extinct, is also one of his forefathers.

The name of the breed was settled in 1880; before then it had been called the Reedwater Terrier and the Coquetdale Terrier. *Mosstrooper*, owned by Miss Mary Rew, was the first Border Terrier registered by the British Kennel Club. The Border Terrier is the smallest of the terriers and also the least fancy. Its owners were perversely pleased their dog was plainer than many of its show-dog cousins, and some fanciers were apprehensive when the British Kennel Club recognized the Border Terrier in 1920. They were worried breeders would try to improve its looks and, in the process, diminish the dog's spunk and stamina, for the Border Terrier was known for running long hours after the fox, then patiently waiting, as long as necessary, by the foxhole to grab the enemy by the throat in its strong jaws and finish the job. Their concern was unnecessary — the Border Terrier has remained the same.

Its head resembles an otter's, with small, V-shaped ears, falling forward close to the cheeks, and dark, keen eyes. A medium-long neck and a straight, quite long and narrow body are set upon strong, rather long legs, with a moderately short tail, carried high, but never curled over the back. The Border Terrier's coat is double: there is a short, thick undercoat and a rough, dense top coat, which protects the dog in the wet, cold countryside. The Border Terrier may be colored red, grizzle and tan, blue and tan or wheaten. A small amount of white on the chest may be allowed. This dog weighs between 11 and 15 pounds.

In addition to running foxes to ground, the Border Terrier will also track badgers, martens, and otters. Although primarily considered a working dog, this frisky, little terrier has become a favorite companion dog, because it is good-tempered, affectionate, obedient and easy to train.

Below: **The spunky and hardworking Border Terrier.** *Right:* **The Bloodhound is known for its wrinkled skin and pendulous ears.**

SELECTING YOUR DOG

Although most dogs are chosen when they come happily bounding up to the prospective owner, some prior thought should be given to selecting the kind of dog you would like. The first consideration is whether you want a purebred dog or a mixed breed. The Humane Society or local pound has dozens of dogs — usually mixed breeds — in need of a home, but a mixed breed dog is an unknown quantity. While this dog may be adorable and devoted to its new owner, it may also have fleas or be sick, or it may grow much larger than your home can accommodate.

If you decide on a purebred dog, you then need to find a breed of dog that is suitable for your personality and home. The suitability of the dog for the house depends chiefly on the amount of exercise it requires as compared with your willingness and ability to supply it. No class of animals varies so in size as the dog, who ranges from the toy of a few pounds to the St Bernard of 250 pounds. Clearly, the housing and exercise requirements of dogs of different sizes differ greatly. The toy could not be allowed to roam about the streets at liberty nor should the St Bernard be confined to the limitations of the small apartment. Being of diminutive size and delicate construction, the toy breeds are well adapted to smaller living arrangements since they require a minimum amount of exercise. Dogs such as the smaller terriers also make excellent city pets. They are small, compact and built low to the ground, and for this reason require only a limited amount of exercise. Large dogs should be left out of consideration when selecting a pet for the apartment, unless the owner is willing to provide the dog with numerous romps in a park. Where a yard can be supplied for the dog, the choice of breed can be considerably broadened.

In addition to size, the color and length of the coat should be considered when selecting a breed. The long-haired dog is bound to be a nuisance about the house while it is shedding. This process is, at best, prolonged, and the hairs attach themselves to the carpets, chairs, and clothes, and are not readily removed. During this period the coat looks rough and detracts much from the animal's appearance. For some owners, white dogs are less desirable because they must be bathed much

The Shetland Sheepdog *(below)* **is a good choice for families seeking a loyal, affectionate dog.** *Right:* **The American Staffordshire Terrier is also good with children.**

more frequently than dogs of a dark color. This is not only troublesome, but may pave the way for skin diseases.

After deciding upon the breed that is most suitable, the next consideration is the proper age at which the dog will be acquired. Even those who do not care for dogs find it hard to resist the mischievous and playful pup, and most people naturally want to adopt a puppy. During the first year the dog passes through the most interesting period of its life. When reared in the household, the puppy becomes much more attached to its masters than does the dog that is brought in as a mature animal. When young children are to play with the dog it is better that the dog become used to them while still young. In addition, the dog can be more satisfactorily trained as a puppy. The health of the grown dog depends a great deal on the way he is cared for during the first year, and no puppy that has had improper treatment will ever attain the same development it might have reached if it had had the proper start.

Nonetheless, there are as many arguments against buying the dog while a puppy as there are for it. During the early weeks of its life, the puppy is very frail and susceptible to outside influences. At weaning time it is often hard to get food which will properly agree with his system, and puppies are sometimes infested with worms. From three to four months puppies frequently suffer from indigestion, worms, rickets, and eczema, all of which, though not particularly dangerous if attended to, may, when neglected, prove fatal. However, if a dog has had proper care, at the age of one year it should be a vigorous, healthy specimen, possessing sufficient resistance to combat disease successfully. If the dog has not had the care, its condition will show it. If the dog has suffered from rickets, the ailment will have been entirely overcome or otherwise be so noticeable that the most casual observer will recognize it. The dog will have attained his full development and any faults will be in full evidence. For these reasons, some people prefer to adopt a dog that is from ten months to one year of age. In general, it is unwise to take in a dog over three years old. At best its lifespan is short, and if early years are already spent the dog rapidly declines into old age.

A final — and obvious — consideration in choosing your dog is selecting a healthy one. The person who has had considerable experience with dogs will be able to determine this with fair accuracy, but the first-time owner might be wise to have a veterinarian examine the animal before it is accepted. But whatever kind of dog you choose, its love and devotion is sure to make it a welcome addition to your home.

Toy dogs, like the Pomeranian *(below)* **and the Yorkshire Terrier** *(right)*, **make good pets for city dwellers.**

BOSTON TERRIER

The Boston Terrier has been called 'The American gentleman among dogs,' because it a native American dog and because it has such a gentle disposition. This dog is courteous to all and carries itself with ease and grace. Its black and white or brindle and white coloring looks a bit like a tuxedo, and its face, white shirt and spats are always sparkling clean, for this small, short-haired canine is immaculate.

In America, the Boston Terrier's ears are cropped to a point, adding to its natty appearance; whereas in England, the ears are left as is, but must stand erect. The Boston Terrier has a broad, flat head and wide-set, large, round dark eyes, with a sweet and intelligent expression. Its well-knit stylish body resembles that of a terrier, while the fairly large head and straight or corkscrew tail are more like the Bulldog's.

Although the Boston Terrier was originally bred for dog fighting, today it is a playful pet. Its ancestors include the English Bulldog and the English Bull Terrier, and probably the French Bulldog and the Boxer, so this is an American dog with English and French blood. From the terrier, the Boston gets its liveliness and fondness for play, and from the Bulldog its courageous and gentle nature.

The Boston Terrier, bred in Boston, born in the USA, was admitted to the stud book of the American Kennel Club in 1893, and is one of only a dozen or so breeds wholly developed in the United States, where it is among the 25 most popular dogs. During the 1920s, the breed was so much in vogue that 20 to 30 percent of the dogs entered in shows were Boston Terriers. Its heyday may have passed, but this likeable little Bostonian is still appreciated in many countries as an affectionate and amusing companion or as an obedient show dog.

The Boston Terrier's ears can be cropped *(below)* or left in their natural bat shape *(right).*

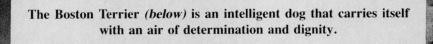

The Boston Terrier *(below)* is an intelligent dog that carries itself with an air of determination and dignity.

BOUVIER DES FLANDRES

In the last century, this large, shaggy dog, with alert eyes and ears, was often seen driving herds of cattle from grazing lands to slaughter pens. During this trip to market, which could take several days in foul weather, the drover depended on his dog to keep the cattle together and moving down long, lonely country roads, and the Bouvier, without waiting for a command, instinctively nudged any strays back into the herd.

The Bouvier des Flandres is a large dog with an especially impressive appearance. It has a powerfully built, compact body with a short, broad back and large head. Upon its body is a very rough coat of thick, wiry and tousled-looking hair which comes in the colors of brown, black, grey, salt and pepper, brindle, and fawn (some Bouviers also have a white star on their chest). The hair forms a full beard and moustache on the face, and makes for long eyebrows over the Bouvier's dark, brown eyes. It has high-set ears, usually cropped, and a docked tail.

Dog fanciers made several attempts to name this Franco-Belgian dog before deciding on the name Bouvier des Flandres. They called it Vuilbaard (dirty beard), Koehond (cow dog), and Toucheur de Boeuf or Pic (cattle driver), but Bouvier des Flandres (cowherd of Flanders) most accurately described the big dog, since it started its career as a cowherd and came from the east and west provinces of Flanders. The first official standard for the Bouvier des Flandres was adopted in August 1912, by the Société Royale St. Hubert.

At the time of the Great War, the intelligent and brave Bouvier served as a messenger under fire and helped find the wounded on the battlefield. The dog was so indifferent to danger that it frequently was killed in the line of duty, and the breed barely survived. Twenty years later, the Bouvier was recruited again to perform the same functions during the Second World War, and once more, owing to its great courage, almost became extinct. Fortunately, a Belgian army veterinarian was able to save a few dogs and started breeding them after the war. They were brought to the United States in the 1930s by a movie producer named Louis de Rochement, and since then have gained in popularity.

Today, the Bouvier still makes an excellent farm dog, but it is also widely used as a guide dog for the blind, and as a police dog. In Belgium, a prize in police work (or similar work) is required of the Bouvier before it can receive the title of champion. The Bouvier serves as a good watchdog because it is exceptionally alert. Because of its docile temperament, however, it does not make a very good guard dog. Although wary with other dogs, the Bouvier gets along well with children and is an ideal family dog. The Bouvier does best in the country or the suburbs, but, if given enough exercise, can adapt to the city. Perhaps because of its natural herding instincts, the Bouvier generally prefers to keep close to home.

These pages: **The trademark of the Bouvier des Flandres is its rough and tousled coat.**

BOXER

It is thought the Boxer got its name from its manner of fighting—The dog appears to box with its front paws. Other theories are that Boxer is a corruption of the German word *Beiszer*, as in Bullenbeiszer (bullbiter or bullbaiter), one of its forbears, or that the Brabanter, now extinct, also called the Boxl, was another ancestor and contributed its name.

Whatever the source of its name, the Boxer is descended from those old war dogs, the Molossus of Epirus and the Tibetan Mastiff, and cousin to the Spanish Alano, the Dogue de Bordeaux and others, while its immediate ancestors were the Bullenbeiszer and the Barenbeiszer, crossed by German breeders in 1850 to achieve certain carefully selected traits. Their aim was to develop the perfect police dog—a fierce and fearless fighter when aroused, but also intelligent and trainable, squarely and strongly built, but light and agile enough to pursue a fast fleeing criminal across fields and over fences and high walls. That they achieved their goal is proven by the Boxer's use in police work in Germany to this day.

Before being perfected toward the end of the nineteenth century, the Boxer was used for bullbaiting and dogfighting, until those sports were outlawed. Like the Boxer, the Bulldog's first career was as a bullbaiter, and there is reason to believe there is Bulldog blood in the German dog, along with some terrier strain. Reinagle's portrait of a Bulldog, done in 1803, shows a dog similar to the Boxer, and pictures of some English dogs of 1850 strongly resemble the Boxer.

The German breeders, however, wanted their creation to look less menacing than the Bulldog, and in a sense they succeeded, for the Boxer has been described as 'a dog of most beautiful ugliness.' American breeders place great emphasis on the Boxer's head, seeking a lean and unwrinkled skull in proper proportion to the strong, muscular body, with tall, straight front legs and well-angulated rear legs.

While the Boxer's tail must be docked, its ears may be cropped or uncropped, depending on the standards in a particular country. Canada and the United States neither ban nor frown on ear-cropping. Those in favor of cropped ears claim this is a simple operation when performed on a young dog under general anaesthesia. Fighting dogs' ears were originally cropped to prevent them from getting torn in battle.

Below: A Boxer puppy. *Right:* The square, well-developed muzzle is one of the Boxer's most distinctive features.

In addition to being an assistant crime-buster, this strong, brave dog served as messenger and medical aide on the battlefields in both World Wars, and since then has worked as a guard dog and as a guide dog for the blind. The Boxer was introduced to England and America when returning military personnel brought the dogs home with them, and soon became very popular in both countries. The breed's popularity is doubtless due to its intelligence, devotion and good nature, along with its playful personality. The Boxer is boisterous and loves roughhousing to an advanced age. It can also be a bit stubborn, so owners need to adopt a no-nonsense approach when training the Boxer.

BRIARD

The Briard is a very ancient breed of French herding dog, which descends from the original European shaggy dog. It is believed Charlemagne had one, based on depictions in eighth century tapestries. Then, in the fourteenth century, Gaston Phoebus described a white, rough-coated dog similar to the Briard in a hunting treatise. A hundred years later, Andrea Mantegna painted the Martyrdom of Saint Sebastian and added two dogs resembling the Briard. In the nineteenth century, the long-haired Briard and the short-haired Beauceron were considered the same breed, until one Abbé Rozier differentiated between the two breeds in 1809. These two French herding dogs made their official debut in 1886 at the Paris Dog Show, but it was not until 1925 that an official standard, sponsored by the French club Les Amis du Briard, was approved, only to be amended in 1930.

Although Briards are referred to as the *Chien Berger de Brie* (Shepherd Dog of Brie), it has not been proven that the breed originated in the Province of Brie, as the name suggests. Instead, many fanciers believe *Chien de Brie* is a corruption of Chien d'Aubry from the fourteenth century legend of *Aubry of Montdidier*. In that story, Aubry's dog, thought to be a Briard, is the central character.

The Briard was renowned for its ability to look after vast flocks of sheep, defending them against wolves and poachers. Two or three dogs were enough to keep watch over 600 to 700 sheep, and they rarely signalled the shepherd for help. As the land was broken down into smaller parcels and the population increased, the Briard's work became more peaceful; it was merely required to keep the sheep on its master's land and guard his property.

The Briard has also been used as a tracking and hunting dog, and during the First World War performed a variety of duties at the front line, such as carrying ammunition and other supplies, acting as guard to warn of surprise attacks and locating wounded soldiers. Records from witnesses state that the Briard had an excellent ability to lead medical corpsmen to the wounded on the battlefield, and would pass by those certain to die.

Originally, the Briard's ears were cropped so that there would be as little lobe as possible for the wolves and other dogs to grasp when a fight was inevitable to save the flock. Generally, most standards today accept the ears cropped or natural, so it is up to the individual owner to make the choice. From its large, fairly long head to its tail with a *crochet*, or hook, at the tip, the Briard is well put together. Long hair forms eyebrows over its dark, rather large eyes, which have a gentle expression, and a moustache and a beard decorate its muzzle, with a large, black nose in the middle. The Briard's long, wavy, goatlike coat, which comes in all colors but white, covers a broad and deep brisket, level back, and slightly sloped croup. The dog is as tall as it is long, measuring between 21 and 27 inches at the withers, and has well-muscled legs and a characteristic second set of dewclaws on its hind legs.

The Briard's gait has been described as quicksilver, which allows it to change course on the spur of the moment, to glide over the ground with all the grace of a large cat. The Briard carries out his work at a trot or a gallop, changing speeds as needed. This is an intelligent, sensitive, loving dog, so eager to please it may overwork itself to exhaustion if not stopped. The Briard—which has been characterized as 'a heart wrapped in fur'—requires an owner willing to give it affection and regularly groom its coat.

These pages: **The Boxer.**

BRITTANY SPANIEL

The Brittany Spaniel, which was named for the French province in which it originated, is unique in that it is the only pointing spaniel recognized by the AKC, and is most often born tailless or with a short tail. If born with a long tail, it is docked to four inches.

This excellent hunting dog was developed by crossing the French Spaniel with the English Setter, probably many centuries ago. It is unclear whether early records are referring to Britannia in France or Bretagne, meaning the British Isles. Oppian, who lived about 150 AD, described the people of Britannia or Bretagne as uncivilized, but commented that their dogs were endowed with superb noses, a trait still possessed by Brittanys.

Brittany-type dogs frequently appear in French and Flemish paintings and tapestries of the seventeenth century, suggesting the dog was popular all along the northern coast of France and Holland, and even in Germany, where the Wachtelhund may be a modern descendant.

In 1850, the Reverend Davies wrote about a hunting trip in Carhaix in the company of small, short-tailed dogs with longer coats than pointers, and which worked well in the bushes. This description fits the Brittany very well. It has also been advanced that the spaniels of Brittany and the setters of England got together when the British setter owners visited France in woodcock season at the turn of the century. *Boy*, an orange and white, was registered as the first *l'epagneul breton (queue courte naturelle)*, but the parenthetic part of the name was soon dropped, in keeping with the deleted requirement for the natural bobtail.

The Brittany was first introduced into the US in 1931 and was recognized by the AKC in 1934. Up to 1 September 1982, this breed was registered as the Brittany Spaniel, but because he works game like a setter, has longer legs than the spaniels, and has high set ears, as opposed to lobular ones, 'Spaniel' was deleted from the name. The American Brittany Club, in 1942, the year of its founding, clarified the French standards for the breed, and they are the same in both countries today, except that the French recognize more colors than the AKC, which allows just two — liver or orange and white, in clear or speckled patterns. More than 150 Brittanys became Dual Champions (in both field and show) in the first 30 years of competition.

This intelligent, hard-working dog has become very popular in the United States as a sporting dog. The fact that it eagerly makes its way through brambles and thickets and points birds like a setter so that they do not fly away before the hunter is within range fulfills the needs of the American bird hunter. The Brittany's smaller size makes it more adaptable to city living, and his fine nose and willing nature are also much appreciated. The sweet-tempered, affectionate and sensitive Brittany requires gentle handling, but innately wants to please its owner and can be easily trained by a careful person. The Brittany is medium-sized, 17.5 to 20.5 inches in height and weighs 30 to 40 pounds. It is compact and stocky, and its coat is dense, either wavy or flat.

BRUSSELS GRIFFON

A street urchin to start with, the Brussels Griffon won the favor of the royal Belgian court when Queen Henrietta Marie, in 1870, took great interest in the breed, an interest which Queen Astrid shared after her.

Although his origin is in question, the modern Brussels Griffon is believed by most to be the product of a union, in the early years of the nineteenth century, between the German Affenpinscher and the Belgian street dog called *Chien Barbe* (Bearded Dog) or *Griffon d'Écurie* (Stable Griffon). All indications point to one distinct type of dog during that era, which was used to catch rats in stables where hansom cabs were kept, and these little dogs, perched next to the coachmen, would ride about the city. Eventually, they became guard dogs and barked at people in the street as they rode by.

At some later date the smooth-coated Pug entered the picture, and this crossbreeding resulted in two types of coat — smooth and rough — which occur even in present-day litters. Those puppies born with smooth coats are termed *Petit Brabançon* and those with the rough coats are the true Brussels Griffons. The Ruby Spaniel was another late participant in creating the modern Brussels Griffon, and this small canine with the winning personality, in large measure, owes its facial characteristics to its spaniel ancestor.

There are people who say the Brussels Griffon dates back much further than the nineteenth century, citing Jan van Eyck's painting of the gentleman Arnolfini and his wife in 1434, which includes a dog that is an exact copy of a Griffon. Based on paintings by Jacopo du Empolic, executed between 1554 and 1640, it is thought Henry III of France owned dogs resembling Griffons.

The Brussels Griffon is intelligent and has a knowing expression on its face. This dog carries its stocky body smartly and is always alert. 'Insouciance' is the Brussels Griffon's middle name and, although rare outside of its native Belgium, owners there enjoy its whiskery appearance and friendly, yet independent, personality.

The Brussels Griffon comes in rust, black and tan, black and rust, tan, or clear red. It is a well muscled, short, compact little dog with a large, round skull, short, broad muzzle and undershot mouth. Its eyes are big, dark and expressive and the ears, sometimes cropped, are as small as possible and carried high, as is the tail, which is docked to one third its natural length. Griffons weigh eight to 10 pounds. The American Kennel Club standard disqualifies a Brussels Griffon with a butterfly nose, hanging tongue or an overshot jaw.

Because they reproduce seldom and only with extreme difficulty, breeders choose the smallest male Griffon and match him with the largest female, in an effort to compensate for the very large heads on the puppies, which may cause delivery problems. Caesarian births are the norm, and often just one puppy is produced. During the first three weeks Griffon pups are fragile and may or may not survive.

BULLMASTIFF

As told in the novels of Charles Dickens, in Victorian England many people were poor and hungry, and to keep food on the table, resorted to poaching on Britain's vast estates. If caught, the penalty was hanging; therefore, rather than risk being apprehended, lawbreakers would kill the gamekeeper.

For protection, gamekeepers needed a special kind of dog. The Mastiff had the size and courage required, but was lacking in speed and agility; the Bulldog, then taller and more like a Boxer in appearance, was overly fierce and too light. Crossing the two produced the ideal dog — the Bullmastiff, originally referred to as the Gamekeeper's Night Dog. To accompany them on their late-night rounds gamekeepers finally had a dog with a good nose, that helped them find the intruder, remained silent as the poacher approached, then fearlessly and aggressively attacked on command, yet was controlled enough to pin the poacher down without mauling him.

The Brussels Griffon (*below and right*) has a thick-set, square body. This tiny breed is fiercely independent.

Between 1860 and 1924, when the British Kennel Club officially recognized the Bullmastiff, breeders worked at creating the perfect anti-poaching dog. The foundation ingredients were 60 percent Mastiff and 40 percent Bulldog, and the descendants of three generations of dogs which were neither pure Mastiff nor pure Bulldog were registered as Bullmastiffs.

Only the strongest puppy from each litter was entered into the breeding program, and for the first four months of its life it was pampered and didn't go to school at all. Then the puppy was introduced to other household dogs and farm animals, and taught to accept their presence, but to keep a distance from them. This was to insure that the dog would not be distracted by other animals.

Next the dog was put through a training course comparable to that of a Marine recruit. It learned to listen to gun shots without flinching, to climb walls, leap over ditches and swim rivers. When it was eight months old, it was muzzled and instructed to go find a man in the countryside. Upon being greeted with blows from a club, the unsuspecting rookie quickly realized it must knock the man down to avoid being knocked down itself. This lesson was repeated with the man swinging his club more and more viciously so that the dog had to work harder and harder to subdue him. After 18 months of training, the Gamekeeper's Night Dog was awarded its diploma.

A publication, called *The Field*, dated 20 August 1901, contains the following story about an early Bullmastiff:

'Mr Burton of Thorneywood Kennels brought to the show one Night-Dog (not for competition), and offered any person one pound who could escape from it while securely muzzled. One of the spectators who had experience with dogs volunteered and amused a large assembly of sportsmen and keepers who had gathered there. The man was given a long start, and the muzzled dog slipped after him. The animal caught him immediately and knocked down this man the first spring. The latter bravely tried to hold his own, but was floored every time he got on his feet, ultimately being kept to the ground until the owner of the dog released him. The man had three rounds with the powerful canine, but was beaten each time and was unable to escape.'

Brindle was the color preferred at first, because it blended in best with the surroundings, making the dog less visible, but the larger proportion of Mastiff blood contributed many light fawn genes, so there are a large number of dogs of that color, as well as red dogs. The Bullmastiff is big, strong, powerful, symmetrically built and active, weighing between 90 and 130 pounds and standing 23 to 27 inches tall. Its head is a large square, and when its dark eyes are alert the dog wrinkles its forehead. The Bullmastiff has a short, broad, dark-colored muzzle with a level or slightly undershot mouth, and a black nose. Its ears are V-shaped and worn close to its cheeks. This large, athletic dog has served in the army, worked for the police and is currently employed as a watchdog by the Diamond Society of South Africa. Today, the Bullmastiff has evolved into a gentle family pet whose appearance alone scares would-be intruders away.

BULL TERRIER

Known as 'the White Cavalier' from its days as a valorous, professional battler, and for its glistening white coat, the Bull Terrier today is an affectionate companion and guard dog. After bullbaiting was abolished in 1835, fans of this bloody sport turned to dogfighting and this led to the creation of the Bull Terrier, for handlers soon realized they needed a faster moving animal with a livelier disposition and a longer muzzle for better biting power. They therefore crossed their Bulldogs, whose strength and ferocity they wanted to preserve, with the now extinct English Terrier. This recipe resulted in the Bulldog Terrier or the Bull and Terrier. A few years later they seasoned the mixture with some Spanish Pointer blood to increase the size of their gladiator.

About 1860, spurred on by fashionable youths of the time, James Hinks, a Birmingham dog dealer, set out to produce an all-white dog. To achieve his aim, it is thought he added Dalmatian, Greyhound and Whippet blood to the original recipe and then interbred the offspring. The breed was officially recognized in 1888, and the Bull Terrier Club of England was formed that same year. Eventually, dogfighting, too, was banned, and Bull Terrier fanciers

decided to save the breed as a companion dog. Because the Bull Terrier tolerates tropical climates well, it became a favorite with the British Civil Service in Africa and India.

In the 1920s, owing to the white dogs' propensity to be born deaf, some color was introduced into the breed, so that there are two varieties of Bull Terrier: the white, which is allowed to have markings on the head, and the colored, which may be any color but white, or any color with white markings, with brindle being the preferred color. The Bull Terrier's coat should be short, flat, harsh to the touch, and have a fine gloss.

The Bull Terrier's long, egg-shaped head and piercing, triangular-shaped eyes have long delighted cartoonists. In addition, it has small, thin, erect ears, a muscular neck, a broad brisket and chest, a short, well-muscled back, straight front legs, and well-developed hindquarters.

Early in the twentieth century, attempts were made to create a Miniature Bull Terrier from small specimens of Bull Terrier. At first, breeders tried to keep the weight so low that few survived. Then in the 1920s, by gradually increasing the dog's weight to about 20 pounds, they succeeded in producing a true and viable miniature of the larger dog, which weighs between 35 and 60 pounds.

Bull Terriers need strong owners who can carefully discipline them. While they are exceedingly loyal to their owners, and will defend them without a thought to their own safety, they can be aggressive and vicious toward strangers, and, if treated brutally, they become extremely dangerous.

These pages: **The Bull Terrier's temperament is characterized as full of fire yet sweet. The breed recently gained popularity in the United States following its use in a television commercial.**

CAVALIER KING CHARLES SPANIEL

When an American dog fancier, Roswell Eldridge, visited England in 1926 looking for King Charles Spaniels, he discovered that the original type, as depicted by Gainsborough, Rubens and Rembrandt, was fast disappearing. As Oriental toy breeds became fashionable in England, breeders of King Charles Spaniels probably introduced Pugs into the breed, to achieve an animal resembling those from the East. A smaller, snub-nosed, round-headed dog resulted, which was not at all to Mr Eldridge's liking. In an effort to save the breed, as King Charles II knew it, he donated prize money to be awarded at London's Croft's Dog Show, for five years, for the best dog and best bitch of the old type. His contest was a great success. Breeders recreated the breed from the few long-nosed puppies born in short-nosed litters, which had previously been discarded as unsuitable.

To distinguish this new canine from the King Charles Spaniel, it was called the Cavalier King Charles Spaniel. The English Kennel Club recognized the reborn spaniel in 1945 and other kennel clubs soon after that. Owing to its good nature and handsome appearance, the Cavalier King Charles Spaniel has continued to grow in popularity as a house pet.

This graceful, well-balanced, long-haired, little dog weighs between 10 and 18 pounds. It is short and compact with a head that is almost flat between the high-set ears; a turned-up nose, large, dark, wide-set, not prominent, eyes; and well-feathered tail, sometimes docked. The four coat variations remain the same in the two breeds. With the return of the longer nose, the Cavalier King Charles Spaniel regained its hunting ability and is an ideal companion on short hunts in open country.

CHESAPEAKE BAY RETRIEVER

This American dog was born of a dramatic sea rescue when an English brig went aground in Chesapeake Bay, off the coast of Maryland, in 1807. Crew and cargo, including two Newfoundland puppies, were saved by an American ship, the *Canton*. The two pups were named *Canton*, after the rescue ship, and *Sailor*, and were presented to the captain of the *Canton* in gratitude for his hospitality. They grew up to be celebrated retrievers and were bred to local retrievers to improve their ability. Other outcrosses are thought to have been made to Flat- and Curly-Coated Retrievers and possibly to Otter Hounds.

By 1884, when the American Kennel Club was founded, the Chesapeake Bay Retriever had evolved, more or less, into the type of dog which exists today—a big, rugged dog that is an excellent swimmer and retriever of wild ducks. It is often called upon to retrieve in snow and ice, so color and coat are very important: the color ranges from faded tan to shades of brown, blending in with the background, and the coat sheds water owing to oil in the harsh outer layer of fur, while the woolly undercoat helps keep the dog dry and warm. As a further aid to swimming in rough waters, the Chesapeake has webbed feet.

The head of the Chesapeake Bay Retriever is broad and round, with a muzzle of medium length. The clear eyes are yellowish and set wide apart. Like the Labrador Retriever, the Chesapeake has a strong chest, deep and wide. Males weigh 65 to 75 pounds; females weigh 55 to 65 pounds.

Chesapeake Bay Retrievers are intelligent, alert, faithful, and have good dispositions. The American Chesapeake Club, founded in 1918, promotes the breed in all areas of AKC competition.

A charming companion, the Cavalier King Charles Spaniel (*these pages*) is a hunter by nature.

CHIHUAHUA

The Chihuahua, weighing one to six pounds, is the world's smallest dog. There are two varieties: smooth-coated and long-coated. Any color is allowed.

The progenitor of today's Chihuahua is believed to have existed as early as the fifth century, prior to the arrival of the Mayan tribes in Mexico. The Mayans probably used these small dogs as propitiatory sacrifices before death. In the ninth century AD, the Toltecs lived in Mexico and are known to have had a breed of dog called the Techichi, small but not tiny, with a long coat and no bark. Carvings of the Techichi found in the Monastery of Huejotzingo, between Mexico City and Fuebla, show a dog that closely resembles the Chihuahua. In addition, there are relics of this ancient breed in other parts of Mexico, including Chichen Itza in far away Yucatan, and around Tula, close to Mexico City. The Techichi is the ancestor of today's Chihuahua.

K de Plinde, a Mexican breeder and Chihuahua authority, reached the conclusion that the contemporary Chihuahua is a product of the union of the Techichi and the tiny hairless dog brought from Asia to Alaska over the land bridge where the Bering Strait now runs. The little hairless dog is credited with reducing the Chihuahua's size.

After the Aztecs conquered the Toltecs in the thirteenth century, Mexican civilization was brought to a glorious state and gold was plentiful. Dogs owned by rich people were highly prized and pampered while, paradoxically, those owned by the poor were probably used for food. Cortez stormed into Mexico in 1519 and left nothing but devastation. Montezuma was killed and his dogs disappeared for hundreds of years.

The early versions of the modern Chihuahua were described as treasured pets, as well as necessary participants in religious rituals of both the Toltecs and the Aztecs. In Mexico and parts of the United States, the remains of early Chihuahuas have been found buried alongside human bones. When an Aztec died, a dog with a red skin was sacrificed, and the two were burned to ashes together. By this process, the dead person's sins were supposed to be transferred to the dog, which spared the human from divine punishment. The dog's soul would then guide the human soul to paradise.

Tourists discovered the first specimens of the modern Chihuahua about 1850 in the Mexican state of Chihuahua. They soon became very popular, with some dogs bringing more than their weight in gold. Forerunners of the breed were imported to the United States before the turn of the century and crossed with toy terriers, such as the Black and Tan Toy, from which match the smooth-coated variety evolved. By crossing the smooth-coated Chihuahuas with toy breeds, such as the Papillon, the Pomeranian, or the Pekinese, American breeders achieved the long-haired Chihuahua. The little dog with the long fur is identical in all ways with the smooth-coated Chihuahua except for his longer coat.

Adelina Patti, the opera singer, brought attention to the breed when she received a Chihuahua concealed in a bouquet of flowers from the president of Mexico in 1890. In the 1940s Xavier Cugat, the band leader, very often conducted with a Chihuahua cuddled in one arm, and for many people this was their first look at the world's tiniest dog.

The dainty Chihuahua is an alert, cheeky dog with a compact, rectangular body. Its head is round as an apple, with a clear stop and a moderately short, pointed muzzle. The ears and eyes are large and set well apart, and the Chihuahua carries its tail curled over its back. The Chihuahua is intelligent, loyal and affectionate with its owner, but wary of strangers. This tiny dog also prefers the company of Chihuahuas to other breeds of dogs, and functions best in families without small children, for, if teased, it will snap. The Chihuahua does not like to be cold and requires a sweater in the wintertime.

Compare the position of the ears on these dogs. When alert, the Chihuahua holds its large ears erect (right).

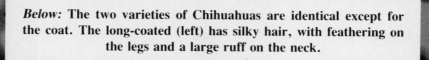

Below: The two varieties of Chihuahuas are identical except for the coat. The long-coated (left) has silky hair, with feathering on the legs and a large ruff on the neck.

CHINESE CRESTED DOG

The Chinese Crested Dog's smooth skin can be as warm as 104 degrees Fahrenheit, and after it has eaten its skin feels warmer. To keep its skin smooth and free from cracks, owners are advised to rub it regularly with baby oil and frequently bathe this small, hairless dog, whose soft, warm skin can be any color or mix of colors. In summer the skin turns darker, probably from exposure to the sun (although it shouldn't be allowed to get sunburned), while in winter it is very sensitive to the cold. If the dog wears a sweater, a cotton garment is preferable to a wool one, as it is allergic to the latter.

Nearly every litter of Chinese Crested puppies contains one or two pups with hair, called 'powder puffs.' Many people believe this is nature's way of keeping the hairless puppies warm. These fluffy pups recur even though they have been excluded from breeding programs. Some breeders think powder puffs strengthen the breed and use them in their programs. A powder puff female will usually produce hairless offspring, so they go for a good price.

An elderly American lady owned the only Chinese Crested Dogs in the world until 1966. Then others began to notice this unusual dog, and selective breeding brought the breed back to life. Today the tiny, finely boned, graceful dog with the silky top knot, large ears, and hairy hare's feet and tail is well established and being introduced in many dog shows. Its feet, which are longer than other dogs' and similar to a hare's, have strong gripping power, almost like a human hand. This alert, intelligent dog makes an excellent house pet, for he is devoted, odorless and does not shed.

Whether the Chinese Crested originated in China is doubted by some experts. They suggest other countries as its place of origin, and certainly hairless dogs have existed not only in China, but in Japan, Africa, the West Indies, and Central and South America as well. The Chinese Crested Dog is, indeed, an ancient breed, and is said to have existed as far back as 1000 BC. It was common in China in the middle of the nineteenth century, but the breed has been extinct there for 50 years.

These pages: **The Chinese Crested Dog. Note the characteristic top knot and hairy feet on the dog** *below.*

DOG CARE

Providing sufficient exercise is the hardest part of the care of the apartment or house dog. In the city the street is about the only available place where the dog can exercise, and for this it needs a harness or collar and a leash. The amount of exercise required by the dog depends directly on its size and temperament and indirectly on the food he consumes. For example, small dogs, such as the Pekingese and Pomeranian, need little outdoor exercise — a walk of five blocks once or twice daily is normally sufficient. Of course the dog that has a yard to romp in requires less attention than one that spends its time indoors. The dog that gets enough exercise and not too much to eat will retain its activity and graceful lines even to old age, while the underexercised and overfed dog grows fat and lazy. The best guide is the condition of the dog. Should the dog begin to gain weight, cut down its food and stimulate a desire to play, keeping the dog active till it tires.

Even though your dog receives the proper food and exercise, it may at times become ill. In general, it is best to consult a veterinarian on the proper treatment, but the owner can prevent potential problems by properly caring for the dog's teeth, ears and nails.

Ordinarily a dog's teeth require little attention. Tartar accumulation may be prevented by cleaning the teeth occasionally, using cotton swabs as a brush and plain water, a solution of table salt or bicarbonate of soda. Likewise, the dog's ears should be cleaned out occasionally. This is best accomplished after the bath in order that no water may be left in the ear. By means of a cotton swab the outer canal of the ear can be cleaned of dirt, discharge and water. If your dog starts to scratch its ear continually — a symptom of canker — a veterinarian should be consulted.

The nails of some house pets grow much faster than they can be worn down and must be occasionally clipped. On the hind legs of many dogs are extra toes, called dewclaws, and since these toes do not touch the ground there is no wear on the nails and they frequently grow so long that they penetrate the skin on the foot-pad. The nails may be regularly filed with a nail file or clipped with heavy shears. In cutting the nails, be careful to avoid penetrating the sensitive structure inside the nail. The nail can be snipped off a little at a time until the dog shows evidence of discomfort.

Because of the high number of homeless or abandoned puppies and dogs, those dogs that are not kept for breeding purposes should probably be spayed or neutered. Your veterinarian can tell you the proper time to have this simple operation performed on your pet.

Below: **The occasional visit to the vet is a necessary part of every dog's life.** *Right:* **A Golden Retriever being X-rayed.**

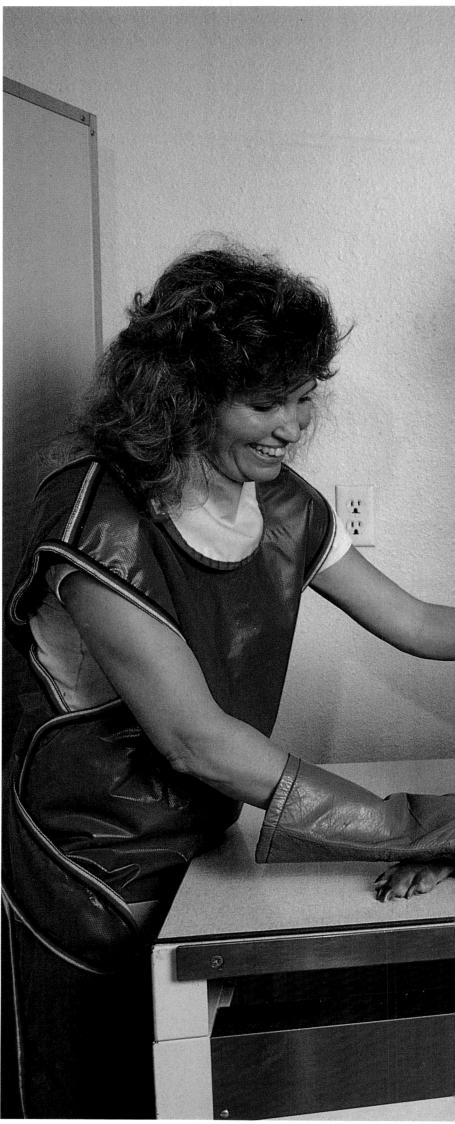

CHOW CHOW

With its dense ruff round its head, the lionlike Chow Chow is an awesome sight in the show ring. The Chow has a profuse double coat with a thick, soft undercoat and a heavy, coarse top coat. Its small, dark eyes have a fierce and forbidding expression and its small, thick, slightly rounded ears are stiff and erect. A blue-black tongue hangs from its mouth. The Chow Chow has a stilted gait caused by straight hocks, and a plumed tail curls gracefully over its back.

A direct descendant of the *Canis palustris*, the probable ancestor of all dogs of the Spitz family, the Chow Chow's structure is similar to that of the oldest fossilized dog — several million years old — discovered in America. The Chow arrived in China with the first settlers from northern Asia and was immediately put to work as a guard dog of herds, sampans and junks, and a hunting dog of sables and other animals. The strongest dogs were harnessed to carts. The Chow was also fattened to be eaten and its fur decorated the coats of many wealthy Chinese women. That the Chow Chow remained a pure breed down through the centuries is evidenced in its portrayal in ancient Chinese art.

The Chinese call this aloof and lordly canine *lang Kou* (wolf dog), *hsiung Kou* (bear dog), *hei she-t'ou* (black-tongued) or *Kwangtung Kou* (the dog of Canton). Chow Chow is pidgin English for food or Oriental bric-a-brac. During the 1700s sailing masters simplified their record keeping by writing down 'chow chow' to cover all cargo—

Below: **A Chow Chow puppy.** *Right:* **An active and alert dog, the Chow has a short, compact and powerfully built body.**

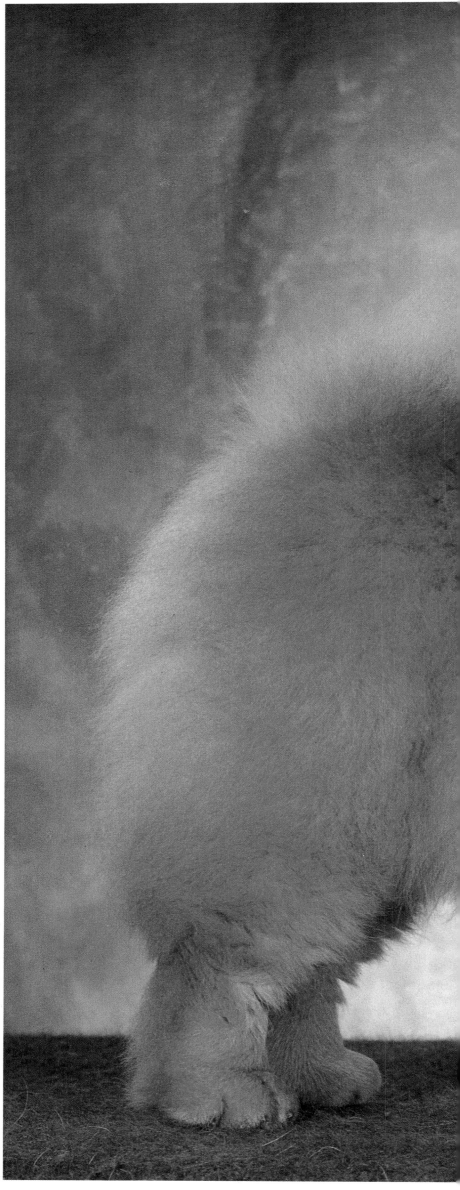

including dogs—and it was at this time that people in the West became aware of the Chow dog, although it had been in existence for over 2000 years. The first Chows that arrived in England were in a zoo.

When the breed was recognized by the Kennel Club in 1894, Queen Victoria took an interest in it, nudging it on its way to popularity. Today, it is one of America's most well-known breeds. The Chow Chow is playful with its owners, but wary of strangers. It does not like to be teased and, if provoked, can be ferocious. A one-owner dog, the Chow is loyal and devoted to those it likes.

CLUMBER SPANIEL

The Clumber Spaniel has been called 'an old man's gundog,' because it moves at a more leisurely pace than Springers or Cockers. Although it is a rather slow worker, the Clumber is resistant to fatigue, persistent and certain to find the game and retrieve it from land or water. The Clumber is known for its distinctive coloring, lemon or orange and white, which permits the hunter to keep the dog in sight, since it works only about 20 yards away; for its rolling gait, which allows it to hunt all day without getting tired; and for hunting in total silence.

This dignified, intelligent, even-tempered dog was developed by the French Duc de Noailles before the French Revolution and became known as a fine retriever. When the revolution began, the Duc brought his dogs to the Duke of Newcastle, at Clumber Park, in Nottingham, whence the breed took its name. The Duke of Newcastle may have crossed these dogs with other breeds.

The Clumber Spaniel's origin is open to speculation. We do know that the Duc de Noailles had been carefully breeding this dog for generations, but no records exist stating which dogs were the ancestors. The long, low body suggests the Basset Hound and the heavy head hints at the Alpine Spaniel, which is related to the St Bernard. These gentle gundogs also look like heavy English Setters with shorter legs, and, of course, docked tails.

Clumbers were first exhibited in England in 1859, at which time this calm, friendly, steady dog became quite popular. By 1883, the breed was registered in the United States.

These pages: **Its dense, lush coat is the Chow Chow's crowning glory.**
Overleaf: **A trio of irresistible Chow puppies.**

COCKER SPANIEL

The Cocker Spaniel is the smallest hunting spaniel and was named either for its special proficiency in hunting woodcock or for its way of cocking, or flushing, game. The large family of spaniels originated in Spain in the fourteenth century, and the name spaniel comes from the word Spain, or España. Spaniels were then used for falconry. Subsequently, they came to be divided into two groups, land spaniels and water spaniels, and the land spaniels were further divided by size, with the cockers and toy spaniels being separated from those of larger dimensions. The toys are primarily kept as pets while Cockers, if trained, enjoy hunting rabbits and flushing other game, although today they are often intended to be merely companions.

The breed was developed in the United States from the English Cocker Spaniel and was first shown in New Hampshire in September 1883. The Cocker Spaniel Field Trial Club started field trials for the breed in 1924. The usual way of hunting with a Cocker Spaniel is to let it cover the territory within gun range, at a quick and lively pace, and, upon flushing the game, the dog should stop, wait for the hunter to fire his shot and then, on command, retrieve.

The Cocker Spaniel differs from the English Cocker Spaniel in several ways. It is smaller — 14 inches for females and 15 inches for males in height, at the withers, compared with 15 to 16 inches for females and 16 to 17 inches for males of the English Cocker Spaniel breed. The Cocker Spaniel has a thicker and longer coat than its cousin, the English Cocker, and has a more cleanly chiselled head with a slightly shorter muzzle. The Cocker Spaniel comes in any solid color including black and any such color with tan points, as well as a particolored variety. The Cocker has large, dark eyes with an alert yet soft and appealing expression, and, like the English Cocker Spaniel, is known for its merry disposition.

These pages: **Since 1982, the Cocker Spaniel has topped the AKC's list of the most popular dogs in the United States.**

COLLIE

With its full ruff and long, flowing coat, the Collie that we know as a beautiful and vivacious companion bears little resemblance to its working ancestors in the Scottish Highlands. Originally bred to herd sheep in Scotland, the harsh coated Collie of yesteryear was the backbone of the sheep industry in Great Britain. Able to do the work of a dozen men, the Collie would run to the distant pasture, round up its flock, separating them from other sheep if necessary and bring them home at just the right pace. If any sheep should take a wrong turn or lag behind, the hearty Collie headed them back in the right direction, all the while guarding its flock against predators. Today most Collies have a less arduous life, and the breed has a much more refined appearance. The bedraggled coat of the sheepherder has been replaced with a luxurious coat, usually black and tan, sable or orange brown with a white frill. The nose is longer, and consequently the head is narrower. The Collie stands 20 to 24 inches and weighs from 40 to 60 pounds. A less well known variety of the breed is the Smooth Collie, which is identical, except for its smooth, short-haired coat.

Star of the big and small screen, the Collie is one of America's most beloved dogs. The original star of the American 1943 film *Lassie Come Home* was actually a male dog by the name of Pal. Pal's descendants, all male, appeared in six sequel films and Pal himself provided the barking for the *Lassie* radio show, which premiered in 1947. So popular was the radio show that Lassie eventually made her way to television from 1954 to 1972, although the canine star once again was always a male. In 1978 Lassie (this time a sixth generation male descendent of Pal) returned to the silver screen in *The Magic of Lassie*, co-starring Jimmy Stewart. While in New York City for personal appearances at Radio City Music Hall, the dog had plush accommodations at the Plaza Hotel in a $380-a-day suite.

Collies *(pages 86 – 89)* have a unique quality that makes people respond to them, and, in fact, show Collies are judged on expression as well as color, size, height and other criteria.

CURLY-COATED RETRIEVER

The Curly-Coated Retriever is one of the oldest of the retrievers. The breed is believed to be descended from the sixteenth century English Water Spaniel, now extinct, with an admixture of some or all of the following breeds: Irish Water Spaniel, Labrador Retriever, St John's Newfoundland and French Poodle, the latter to give his coat a tighter curl.

The Curly was first exhibited at England's Birmingham Show in 1860, and he sailed to New Zealand in 1889, where he is still a popular duck and quail hunting dog. Australian hunters, too, appreciate this steady, tender-mouthed retriever's skill in the water, and he is a star in the swamps and ponds that are part of Murray River. The Curly arrived in the United States in 1907 and was registered with the AKC in 1924.

The Curly-Coated Retriever has a reputation for being easy to train because it is intelligent, even-tempered, affectionate and courageous. He is an all-around retriever, faithful pet and excellent guard dog. The Curly weighs from 70 to 80 pounds and is 25 to 27 inches tall. It has a long, well-proportioned head, large eyes, small pendant ears and a deep, but not wide chest. The coat is a dense mass of curls in black or liver.

DALMATIAN

Countries claiming to be the birthplace of the Dalmatian are as widely spread as the wanderings of the gypsies, with whom the Dalmatian has often been found, and they, doubtless, had a hand in dispersing the dog to a variety of different locations.

No compelling evidence proves he originated in Dalmatia, a region in west Yugoslavia, along the Adriatic, which previously (1815 to 1919) was a province of Austria, although this is the breed's first proved home and the place from which it gets its name. Authorities believe the Dalmatian may be connected to Yugoslavia through the Istrian Pointer, a possible ancestor whose profile resembles the modern Dalmatian. The first references to a Dalmatian are in the mid-eighteenth century.

Antique frescoes and paintings in Egypt and Greece depict dogs similar to the Dalmatian, making those countries contenders for the honor of being the homeland of the spotted dog. Some authorities believe it came from India because it resembles the Bengali Braque, now extinct. They conjecture that the Bengali Braque was crossed with the Bull Terrier and the Pointer to produce the Dalmatian.

Another theory holds that the Dalmatian is descended from the Great Dane, since its coloring is close to that of the Harlequin Great Dane, which would make Germany his place of origin, but few favor this idea. The Dalmatian looks more like the Braque Français, and there are supporters of France as its place of birth. The Danes call

Right: **The Curly-Coated Retriever.** *Below:* **The Dalmatian's spots are black or liver, ranging in size from a dime to a half dollar.**

him the Small Dane, and because there are a great many Dalmatians in Denmark, that country claims the breed as one of theirs.

It was the English, however, who, in the nineteenth century, perfected the breed. Originally, puppies were born with coats of many colors, not just black and white or liver and white. By careful selection of the parents, English breeders succeeded in controlling the coloring of the dogs. The English gave the Dalmatian several nicknames, first and foremost 'Carriage Dog' or 'Coach Dog' because the dog loved to trot beside the carriages and even thread its way among the horses legs without causing them to miss a step. English children dubbed him 'Plum Pudding,' seeing its spots as the raisins in their favorite cake. The Dalmatian was also called the 'Spotted Dick.' In the Gay Nineties, in America, it accompanied horse-drawn fire wagons, and earned the name 'Fire House Dog.'

Although the Dalmatian was a favorite of royalty and the upper classes, it started life as a working dog, and its activities have been as varied as its alleged countries of origin. The Dalmatian carried messages during the Balkan Wars of 1912 and 1913, served as a sentinel on the borders of Dalmatia and Croatia, was a bird dog for the gypsies, a guard dog to protect travelers against highwaymen and a ratter in London's stables and fire houses. The Dalmatian has also been a draught dog, sled dog, shepherd, trail hound, retriever, boar and stag dog (in packs), and circus and stage performer.

But the Dalmatian is most renowned as the one and only coach dog. The Dalmatian has an affinity for horses, and they return its affection; in times past, the Dalmatian was happy sleeping in the stable with its equine friends. The dog is physically made for the road and loves to run. Only the advent of the automobile put an end to its career as a coach dog. Today, it is a picturesque, intelligent and affectionate pet.

Dalmatian puppies are born white, develop their spots between two and five weeks, and reach maturity at a year of age. This is a strong and active dog, well proportioned, with a head of good length, moderate stop and lean lips. Its eyes are round and well apart, with an intelligent expression, and its ears, of medium size, hang loose. A long, slender, arched neck leads to a level back and muscular body set on straight front legs and rounded, muscled hindquarters, with a thick, tapering, slightly curved tail.

DACHSHUND

Three times as long as it tall, the Dachshund combines the qualities of the hound with the terrier and is probably descended from these two types. From its hound ancestors it gets its long ears, and from the terriers its head. Its body and neck are long but muscular, and the legs, though extremely short, are strong and well boned. Most Dachshunds have a short and silky coat, but there are also long-haired and wire-haired varieties. The coat is often a dark red tan, but also brown as well as black and tan. In disposition, the Dachshund's heritage is evident in that it has the self-reliance of the terrier and the affectionate nature of the hound.

The Dachshund is a favorite dog in Germany, where it was used to seek out badgers in their holes. To follow a badger into its hole requires a dog of courage as well as unusual design, and this compact dog fits the bill.

Above: Once seen on horse-drawn fire wagons, the Dalmatian is still identified with the fire engine. *Below:* The Dachshund is courageous, often to the point of rashness. *Right:* A Dachshund puppy.

Below: The three varieties of Dachshunds (from left to right)—shorthaired, wirehaired and longhaired.

DOBERMAN PINSCHER

The 'Dobe' was created by Herr Louis Dobermann, a tax collector and dog breeder of Apolda, in Thuringia, Germany, between 1865 and 1870. As keeper of the local animal shelter, Dobermann had a supply of dogs with which to work. His aim was to produce a dog to protect him while he was out collecting taxes. The dog was to be agile like a terrier and strong like a shepherd. In addition, this guard dog was to be large, intelligent, fast, spirited and fearless.

While no records remain of the dogs Dobermann used in his project, authorities believe the smooth-haired German Pinscher, the Rottweiler, the Manchester Terrier, the Beauceron and the Greyhound all went into the mixture. Other suggestions include the Great Dane, the Black and Tan Terrier, the Schnauzer, the German Shepherd and the Pointer.

People looked askance at the first Doberman Pinschers, whose name comes from the founder of the breed minus one 'n' and *pinscher*, meaning 'terrier' in German. Because they are born guard dogs, it is common for a two-month-old puppy to snarl and show his teeth in a power play. A Swiss breeder, Gottfried Lietchi, commented: 'They were certainly robust, had absolutely no fear, not even of the devil himself, and it required a great deal of courage to own one.'

One of the many Dobie stories told and retold is that an especially fear-inspiring American Doberman won Best in Show three times before any judge had the courage to examine the dog's mouth. At last, at the fourth dog show, a brave judge pried open the dog's mouth and learned there were some teeth missing, which is a serious fault.

Owing to his qualifications as a guard dog, the Doberman was soon noticed by the police and invited to become a police dog. The Doberman worked well in this capacity, and when World War I came along it transferred its talents to the military, serving as a patrol and guard dog at the German front lines. It was also used to guide blind soldiers. During World War II, the US Marines adopted the Dobe as their official war dog. A dog named *Andy* was decorated for saving a tank platoon held down by heavy fire on Bougainville by sniffing out two hidden Japanese machine-gun nests.

The sharp-nosed dogs have since gone into the security business where they search out nighttime prowlers in stores and warehouses and on estates. Despite the Dobe's fiery disposition, if it has an owner who can command its love and devotion, and whom it will obey, the Doberman makes an outstanding companion dog and is beautiful to behold as well. It has been said there are no bad Dobermans, just bad owners. From its cropped ears to its docked tail, with lean, well-muscled body and gleaming coat in between, the Doberman looks more like an aristocrat than most dogs.

In the United States the breed has been fostered by the Doberman Pinscher Club of America, founded in February 1921. Through the efforts of this club, the Doberman is currently near the top of all breeds in registration.

ENGLISH BULLDOG

It has been said that the English Bulldog is so ugly he is beautiful. Certainly the Bulldog is oddly formed, with a huge wrinkled head and gargoyle-like face. Yet the dog is good-natured and kind, likes children, is quick to learn and loves games. The British consider the Bulldog the most distinguished and most British of all canines, and the dog symbolizes the qualities Britons admire most in themselves — bravery, tenacity and levelheadedness.

As its name implies, the Bulldog took its name from the old-time sport of bullbaiting, popular in England for 700 years until it was outlawed in 1835. The object of the dog was to seize the bull (which was tethered to a stake by a 15-foot rope) by the nose, pin it to the ground and hold it there. So that the Bulldog could more easily hold onto the bull, the dog was bred to have an undershot jaw and a retreating nose. The Bulldog was also used for bearbaiting and dogfighting and needed to be quick and active as well as strong. In spite of its menacing appearance and past history, the Bulldog is a gentle and good-natured dog and makes a safe and dependable family pet. If angered, however, the Bulldog's legendary courage and tenacity comes into play, and the dog will fearlessly fight, even to death. Before all the meanness was bred out of him, slightly over a century ago, the Bulldog probably looked more like a coarse, heavy Boxer, weighing 100 pounds or more, with longer legs. When bullbaiting was banned and the Bulldog was no longer needed and in danger of dying out, some enthusiasts united to save the breed, and the Bulldog in it present form was finalized about 1900. The British Kennel Club officially recognized the Bulldog in 1873, and the American Kennel Club a few years later.

As a result of crossbreeding to achieve the desired standard, the Bulldog of today is short-legged, short-winded and short-lived. Weighing 30 to 40 pounds, this dog is stocky and has a large, square head with a deeply wrinkled face. Its neck is thick and short, the shoulders wide and low. The eyes are wide-set and low on the face. Brindle is the preferred color, but white, black and white, fawn, red, brown and even solid black are permissible. The coat is fine, short, bright and smooth.

The Bulldog has served a variety of purposes, from bullbaiter to police dog, from guard dog to aide to the Marines. The Bulldog is even the mascot for the Yale football team.

Below: A courageous fellow, the English Bulldog is never vicious.
Right: The Doberman's expression conveys energy and vigor.

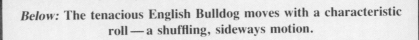

Below: The tenacious English Bulldog moves with a characteristic roll — a shuffling, sideways motion.

ENGLISH COCKER SPANIEL

At one time, spaniels of all sizes were considered one group, for they appeared in the same litters. Then, in the seventeenth century, the larger dogs began to be used to spring game, while the smaller ones were used to hunt woodcock. The former were called Springer Spaniels and the latter Cocker Spaniels (meaning the English Cocker Spaniels), and the Kennel Club of England recognized them as separate breeds in 1892. Developed mainly around Wales and southern England, the English Cocker's popularity spread until, by the mid 1930s, he was Britain's most popular breed, and today he is reasonably well known in the United States.

The English Cocker is sturdy and well balanced, and has a well-developed head 'with no suggestion of coarseness,' according to the AKC standard. Its head does not have as pronounced a stop as does the Cocker Spaniel. Various colors are permissible: solid colors, particolors, black and tan and roan. This dog is also called 'the merry cocker' because of its cheerful, animated, loving personality. As with the Cocker Spaniel, daily brushing and grooming are needed, in addition to professional trimming every eight to 10 weeks.

ENGLISH SETTER

The setter got its name from the manner in which it freezes and positions game. It sits down halfway, flexes its hindquarters, keeps its tail at a slant, and both forelegs, as a rule, remain firmly planted on the ground. When hunting the setter holds its head high so as not to miss the scent of any feathered game. In olden times game was often caught in a net, and the setter crouched, or set, so that the net could be thrown over both dog and game.

The English Setter is the most ancient setter breed; authorities say it was a trained hunting dog in England over 400 years ago. Hans Bols, in *Partridge Shooting and Partridge Hawking*, written in 1582, gives us illustrations of contemporary setters and spaniels, showing the setters with full tails and the spaniels with docked tails. From early writings of sportsmen, there is evidence the old English Setter was developed by crossing the Spanish Pointer, the large Water Spaniel, and the Springer Spaniel.

Two men were instrumental in the development of the modern breed: Edward Laverack and RL Purcell Llewellin. In 1825, Mr Laverack obtained *Ponto* and *Old Moll* from the Reverend A Harrison, who had evidently maintained the breed true for at least 35 years, and started a breeding program, producing some superb specimens: *Prince*, *Countess*, *Nellie*, and *Fairy*. Mr Llewellin bought several of Mr Laverack's best show dogs, which he crossed with some new dogs, known as the Duke-Rhoebes, which he had obtained in the north of England. These matings resulted in some renowned field trial champions, which excited the interest of American and Canadian sportsmen, and soon the English Setter was established in North America. *Count Noble* is a famous foundation dog, whose name appears on many pedigrees.

The English Setter has remained popular over the years because it is beautiful, a fine hunting dog and has a lovable disposition. This aristocratic dog has a slightly wavy, long and silky coat which comes in black and white, lemon and white, orange and white, liver and white or black, white and tan. All-over speckled dogs are preferred to those with large colored spots. Its head is long and lean, with a well-defined stop, and its eyes are dark brown, with an intelligent and mild expression. The English Setter moves easily and gracefully, and is happy in the field or as a pet in the suburbs.

Below: **An English Setter puppy.** *Right:* **The English Setter carries its head proudly.**

ENGLISH SPRINGER SPANIEL

This happy dog with the friendly face and good disposition is valued by sportsmen for its versatility as a hunting dog and a charming companion. Bounding merrily back and forth, in front of the hunter, head and tail held high, ears flopping in the wind, the English Springer Spaniel flushes pheasant, ruffled grouse and woodcock from their brushy cover. Then, after waiting and watching where the downed bird has landed, it goes to retrieve it on land or in water, in fair weather or foul. Should it come upon a rabbit, the dog will spring that, too, and it may stop, momentarily, to point a butterfly.

About six hundred years ago, in England and France, spaniels of varying sizes worked with Greyhounds and falcons, as well as huntsmen with nets. They would chase the birds from the woods and underbrush to be caught by the Greyhounds and falcons, or the hunter's net. Until the early years of the nineteenth century there was little to no distinction made among the different sporting spaniels. From that time on, however, fanciers began selective breeding to perfect a land spaniel of medium size. By the 1850s, these keen sportsmen had produced the prototype of the present-day English Springer Spaniel. They added the adjective 'springer' to the name in recognition of the dog's special sporting skill. The Kennel Club of England accepted the breed for registration in 1902, and the American Kennel Club in 1927.

Eager to please and easy to train, the Springer has kind, alert eyes in a beautiful head, which should be about the same length as its neck, and blend in with its neat, sturdy body and docked tail. The coat of this symmetrical dog may be any of the colors recognized for hunting spaniels: liver and white, black and white, tricolor, including tan markings (usually on the eyebrows, cheeks, inside the ears, and under the tail), blue or liver roan. On the ears, chest, legs and belly, the Springer has fine, feathered hair of moderate length. The hair on its head, the front of its forelegs, and below its hocks is short and soft, and its body coat is dense, flat, moderately long and thorn and waterproof.

ENGLISH TOY SPANIEL

Although this affectionate, little spaniel is considered an English breed, it probably originated in Japan or China, perhaps lived for a time in Spain and was certainly well known in France before arriving in England in the 1500s. From the time of its appearance in Europe, the toy spaniel became a great favorite of royalty.

Toy spaniels appear with noble ladies in paintings of the Renaissance, but they do not look exactly like the contemporary English Toy Spaniel — or King Charles Spaniel, as he is called in England — because at a later period dogs from China and Japan were bred in, causing the breed to become smaller and to have a domed head with a shorter, turned-up nose. The Cavalier King Charles Spaniel is a twentieth century recreation of the original English Toy Spaniel, as shown in the paintings of Titian and Veronese.

It was the custom of court ladies to keep little animals under their voluminous skirts to keep warm in the wintertime, and even austere Elizabeth I enjoyed the company of the 'delicate, neat and pretty kind of dog called the Spaniel Gentle, or the comforter.' When Mary Queen of Scots returned from France to become Queen of Scotland, she brought several of these dogs with her. An English Toy Spaniel accompanied her to the scaffold in 1587, and stayed with her till the end, showing the small dog's devotion.

King Charles II (1660–85) cherished the black-and-tan variety so much that Toy Spaniels of this color are called King Charles Spaniels. He kept a large number of them as pets and took them everywhere with him. Pepys, the diarist, criticized the King for playing with his dogs instead of attending to his royal duties. In addition to the King's Black and Tans, red-and-white Toy Spaniels soon won favor with John Churchill, first Duke of Marlborough, and became known as Blenheim Spaniels, after the Duke's residence, Blenheim Palace. A tricolored variety was called the Prince Charles, and a solid chestnut red dog was dubbed the Ruby. As late as 1850, Toy Spaniels were used for hunting purposes, but by crossing them with East Asiatic dogs, the hunting instinct was gradually bred out.

Sometimes called a 'Charlie' or a 'Carpet Spaniel,' the English Toy Spaniel has ears so long they almost touch the ground, measuring 20 to 22 inches or more, and a long, wavy, silky coat. It weighs between nine and 12 pounds and has strong, stout legs.

This page: **The English Springer Spaniel stands 19 to 20 inches at the shoulder and weighs 49 to 55 pounds.** *Right:* **A Springer puppy.**

FIELD SPANIEL

The English Field Spaniel was developed toward the turn of the last century by hunters who wanted a slightly heavier bird dog than the Cocker and Springer types. Breeders crossed various spaniels and perhaps added some Basset blood for good measure. Then, just as hunters began to admire the new breed, Victorian exhibitors got carried away and remade the Field Spaniel into a show dog with an overlong body and squat legs, and a high price attached. Sportsmen revolted and refused to buy these 'caterpillar dogs,' as they called them. After World War II, more sensible breeders remodeled the Field Spaniel again, and it became leggier and shorter in body. Now the Field is a symmetrical hunting dog and a capable retriever on land or water.

Usually black, its silken coat is 'as the sheen on the raven's wing,' although it sometimes has a liver, mahogany or red-roan coat with tan trimmings. The Field Spaniel weighs between 35 and 50 pounds and is 18 inches tall at the shoulder. The Field Spaniel is a dependable worker with an even temperament and deserves a wider public.

FINNISH SPITZ

Known as 'the barking bird dog of Finland' for its way of flushing birds (especially wood grouse) with a rousing bark, the Finnish Spitz, or *Suomenpystykorva*, has been raised for centuries in Finland. The Finnish Spitz is mentioned in several heroic national songs and is Finland's national dog.

Some authorities claim the Finnish Spitz is a descendant of the northern wolf, while others contend the dog is not related to the wolf at all, but has as his forebears the Pariah, a half-wild dog found in India, which has a similar body and coat. The latter group asserts the ancestors of the Finnish Spitz were introduced to Scandinavia by Finno-Ugric tribes migrating northwards, and from these dogs came several spitz breeds — the Finnish Spitz, the Norrbotten Spitz, the Norwegian Buhund, and the Puffinhound.

Up to the turn of the century, the Finnish Spitz was used by Lapp hunters for hunting polar bears and elk in Lapland — the northern regions of Norway, Sweden, Finland, and Russia. Finally, travelling southward, large numbers of these canines settled in Finland. In 1927, Sir Edward Chichester brought a pair of Finnish Spitzes to England and the breed was soon recognized by the British Kennel Club. Lady Kitty Ritson, a British breeder, called the dog *Finkie*, a nickname by which the breed is still known today.

Lively is the word which best characterizes this dog — especially its dark, bright eyes, alert ears and tail curled over his back. The standard established in 1892 by Finland's Kennel Club calls far a dog 15 to 20 inches tall at the shoulders, weighing 23 to 36 pounds, with a clean-cut head and almost square body. The Spitz has a long, dense double coat which is colored red brown or red gold.

Its hunting ability is honored each year in Finland by a competition held to select the Finnish Spitz that is the best hunting dog. This courageous, fearless, faithful and friendly dog also makes a good companion and guard dog.

FLAT-COATED RETRIEVER

The Flat-Coated Retriever is the straight-haired twin of the Curly-Coated Retriever. They both come in black or liver and have such similar standards that some authorities consider them to be varieties of the same breed. The Flat-Coated Retriever, however, has a slightly lighter build.

A common ancestor of the two breeds is the Newfoundland, which was brought to British ports by Canadian seafarers during the last two

Right: **A Flat-Coated Retriever relaxes at home.**

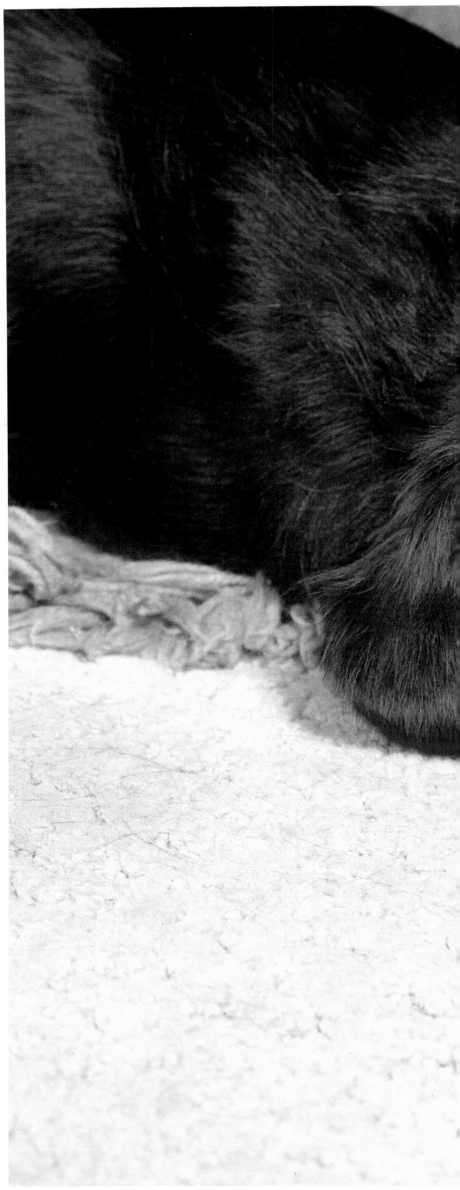

centuries. To create the Flat-Coated Retriever, Collie blood was introduced to increase the dog's stamina as a working dog and Setter blood to improve his scenting ability. The prototype of today's Flat-Coated Retriever was shown in Britain about 1860, and over the next 20 years, by careful breeding, the breed was perfected. It was a popular show dog and sporting dog up to the First World War, at which time the breed was superceded in popularity by the Labrador and the Golden Retriever. When the Flat-Coated Retriever was chosen Supreme Champion at Croft's in 1980, new attention was attracted to the breed; however, this beautiful dog remains rather rare.

This handsome, intelligent, affectionate dog weighs 60 to 70 pounds, has a long head, square muzzle, brown eyes, small pendant ears, straight forelegs and dense, fine, slightly wavy, medium-length hair.

FRENCH BULLDOG

The French Bulldog, or *Bouledog Français*, has two distinctive features: bat ears and a uniquely shaped skull. The skull should be level between the ears, with a domed forehead. American fanciers are responsible for preserving the bat ears, since the tendency in the mid nineteenth century was toward rose ears. Through their persistence, the sweet-tempered, frisky French Bulldog maintained its individuality and did not become a miniature English Bulldog.

The origin of the French Bulldog is in question. One group believes that English lace-makers from the English Midlands took their Bulldogs with them when they moved to France for better job opportunities in the last century, and there the British dog was crossed with other, smaller dogs until he became smaller and gentler. Others, basing their claim on an ancient bronze plaque, dated 1625, which depicts a bat-eared dog similar to the French Bulldog, declare him to be a native of Spain because the plaque is inscribed *Dogue de Burgos, España*. Bullfighting certainly took place in Burgos, as it did in most cities in Spain, and *perros de presa*, or dogs of prey, were developed from the Pyrénée Mastiff by Spanish breeders so that the receded nostrils and protruding underjaw would allow the dog to breathe while hanging on indefinitely to the bull's nose. It is thought these dogs went to France, where they were trained to fight donkeys before being shrunk and becoming the *petit divertissement* of fashionable Parisiennes. Still others state that the miniature fighting dogs were born as runts in regular litters in Spain and brought to France as curiosities, where the French crossed them with Miniature English Bulldogs, a breed which the English had tried to popularize without success. The final result was the French Bulldog. Whichever of the three theories is correct, it is certain that the French Bulldog descends from either the English Bulldog or a Spanish dog of bulldog type.

American breeders formed the French Bulldog Club of America and standardized the breed. In 1898, fanciers held a specialty show devoted to the French Bulldog in the ballroom of the Waldorf-Astoria, and these little gnomelike dogs became the *enfants favoris* of society.

The 'Frenchie' today is primarily a pet and watchdog. It is bright and alert, easy to care for owing to its short coat and always ready for a romp with children. Acceptable colors are brindle, fawn, white, and brindle and white. Weight should be under 28 pounds.

Below: The Flat-Coated Retriever is an athletic, energetic dog. *Right:*
The sturdy French Bulldog.

GERMAN SHEPHERD

Despite its somewhat stern appearance, the German Shepherd loves working with people and actually becomes quite lonely if not given regular companionship. For this reason, the German Shepherd excels as a guide dog, a police dog, a military patrol dog, and a watchdog (if not left alone for long periods of time). The German Shepherd is also a very valued companion dog, showing much devotion to its owner or family.

Developed in Germany several hundred years ago, the German Shepherd was originally bred from traditional herding and farm dogs. Formal sponsorship of the breed began in 1899, with the founding of the German dog club *Verein fur Deutsche Schaferhunde*. Although always recognized by the name German Shepherd, dog lovers in England and other United Kingdom countries gave the dog a new name, Alsatian, in order to protect it from anti-German sentiment following World War I. The Alsatian name is still in use in Britain today. The war was also responsible for the German Shepherd's arrival in America, for American soldiers brought the dog home with them after their duty in Europe. The dog is now recognized by the American Kennel Club.

In shape, walk and color, the German Shepherd closely resembles, and is sometimes taken for, a wolf. Strongly built, it has a relatively long body with a deep chest and straight back. Its strong, cleanly chiseled head includes a long, slender muzzle, dark, almond-shaped eyes, and very strong teeth. Its coat is coarse and of two layers: a medium-long, straight and harsh outercoat which lies close to the body, and a short inner coat that varies in thickness with the season. The color of the German Shepherd ranges from white or pale grey to black. Most often, however, it is grey and black or black and tan. In the United States, German Shepherds with strong, rich colors are preferred, and any white dog or dog without a predominantly black nose is disqualified from AKC showing. Completing the wolflike picture are two erect, very high-set ears, and a low-set, bushy tail.

The German Shepherd is an extremely intelligent dog, which is one reason it is so valued in work with humans. Its energetic, keen mind results in trouble, however, if the dog is not kept active. The German Shepherd needs plenty of room and lots of exercise. It does not do well if left alone for long hours, or tied up, or in some other way restricted. Given continual contact with people when a pup, the German Shepherd makes a wonderful pet. Although reserved with strangers — and hostile with strange dogs — the German Shepherd is devoted and gentle with its family, including small children.

The German Shepherd's intelligence is evident at a young age — as seen in the alert expression on the puppy *below*.

GOLDEN RETRIEVER

One of the most beloved companion breeds of all time, the Golden Retriever is a keenly intelligent, gentle dog with a seemingly limitless amount of affection to give its owners. Friendly, willing and devoted, this popular family pet is good with both children and other pets. It loves to play — especially fetch and carry — and craves being a part of the action.

In addition to being a wonderful companion, the beautiful Golden Retriever is a very versatile dog, performing equally well in the field (tracking and hunting), as a guide dog, and in obedience trials. The first three dogs of any kind to win the American Kennel Club Obedience Champion title, beginning in 1977, were Golden Retrievers.

Originating in England in the early nineteenth century, the Golden Retriever was developed by a man named Sir Dudley Marjoribanks (also known as Lord Tweedmouth) who crossed a yellow, flat-coated retriever with the now extinct Tweed Water Spaniel. The early nineteenth century was a time when game hunting — in particular, the hunting of game birds, both on land and water — was an extremely popular sport in England and Scotland. In creating the Golden Retriever, Sir Dudley was responding to the demand for a new breed of sporting dog that was specialized at retrieving game birds from icy waters. So successful was Sir Dudley that, even today, over a hundred years later, the Golden Retriever is still considered an outstanding hunting dog and is often used to retrieve ducks and upland birds.

As its name suggests, the coat of the Golden Retriever is a rich golden color sometimes referred to as butterscotch. The water-repellent coat is thick, with some wave, and lots of feathering around the neck, forelegs, stomach and the underside of the tail. Because the coat is flat, the Golden Retriever was originally lumped together with the Flat-Coated Retriever and was not recognized as a separate breed until 1913.

Although the Golden Retriever has a short body and broad head, overall its build is well balanced and powerful. In order to maintain its strength, however, the Golden Retriever requires lots of exercise — some say two hours a day — which should frequently include its favorite exercise, swimming.

The friendly Golden Retriever gets along well with people *(below)* as well as kittens *(right)*.

GREAT DANE

Known as the Deutsche Dogge throughout central Europe, the Great Dane — one of the oldest breeds — has been a hunter down through the centuries and in Germany was used in the recent past to hunt wild boar. Because of its size and formidable appearance, the Great Dane makes an effective guard dog, but can also be a good companion if properly trained and exercised. This big dog, however, does have an excitable and sometimes impatient disposition, and therefore does not make a good pet for children.

Although not as swift as a Greyhound, the Great Dane has similar lines, but is much more massive and powerful, weighing between 120 and 150 pounds. Ranging from 28 to 34 inches in height, the Dane is a statuesque and magnificent animal. It has strong, straight legs and back, a long tail and an impressive head with pointed ears.

GREATER SWISS MOUNTAIN DOG

The Greater Swiss Mountain Dog is the largest of the four types of Swiss Mountain Dog, all of which are believed to be descended from the Tibetan Mastiff. A team of Tibetan Mastiffs accompanied the Roman legions on their trek through Saint Gottard to Transalpine Gaul. They were brought along to herd the livestock intended as food for the soldiers, and many stayed in Saint Gottard.

The Greater Swiss, having evolved from the Mastiff, doubtless by mating with local Swiss farm dogs, first appeared in the cantons in the twelfth century. It performed the same tasks as the Bernese — pulled carts, herded cattle and guarded property. In the fourteenth century, the big dog had made some enemies, and an edict was issued by the *bürgermeister* of Zurich, Hans Waldman, for its

extermination. The Greater Swiss was charged with harming game and damaging the vineyards. The peasants, however, refused to turn over their loyal and affectionate herders and companions, and shopkeepers, too, came to the dog's defense, for the Greater Swiss had conscientiously guarded their wares, and as a result the order was never enforced.

This intelligent, easily trained dog makes a fine family pet, provided there is ample space for it to stretch its legs. It weighs 88 pounds or more and has a massive, robust build. Its head is large and powerful and its eyes are dark and alert. High-set ears fold gently on either side of its head. The Greater Swiss's short-haired coat is black, tan and white, and it stands tall on well-muscled legs and wears its tail long. As a guard dog, it is said the Greater Swiss never sleeps, is always attentive, and ready to spring up at the smallest noise, and as a herder has the reputation of recognizing each animal in the herd it is tending.

GREYHOUND

Fastest of all dog breeds, the Greyhound is able to reach speeds of up to 35 miles an hour and cover 18 feet of ground in one running stride. So fast is the Greyhound that an organized sport — Greyhound racing — has been developed around the breed.

Streamlined and slender, the Greyhound looks like it was built for speed. Aerodynamically, from head to tail, the Greyhound is perfectly suited to run like the wind. Beginning with a narrow head and pointed muzzle, the well-proportioned body continues with a long neck, a deep chest, a slender, wasp waist, an arched back, long, powerful legs and a long, slim tail. Even the Greyhound's ears are aerodynamically designed: When a Greyhound races, the ears fold flat against its neck just like the flaps on a departing plane.

Although now noted for speed, the Greyhound was not always a racing dog. One of the oldest breeds, the Greyhound probably

Below: Size and temperament combine to make the Great Dane truly a majestic dog. *Right:* The fleet-footed Greyhound.

originated in Egypt between 4000 to 3500 BC and was developed as a hunting dog. So valued was the dog that its likeness is found on many Egyptian tombs. The Greyhound also hunted for the ancient Greeks, Persians and Romans. By the ninth century, dogs similar to the Greyhound were hunting rabbits, deer, foxes and other small game in the British Isles. Seven hundred years later, the Greyhound arrived in North America, brought over by Spanish conquistadors.

Because the Greyhound hunts by sight and not by scent (the Greyhound has no scenting ability), the ancients named the dog, the 'gaze hound.' The exact origin of the Greyhound name, however, is not known. Some say it comes from the old English word *grech*, which means dog. Others claim it comes from the word *Greece* (*Gracius*). Another, longer theory says that only men of degree were allowed to own the dog and so they became known as degree hounds. Over time, this became gree hounds, and then, finally, Greyhounds. Because the dogs are not only grey — their short, smooth coat can be tan, brindle, white, black, bluish or red — it is unlikely the Greyhound name refers to its color.

The Greyhound's passionate and competitive spirit makes it a popular dog around the world. Today, coursing meets for Greyhounds are held in Australia, England, Ireland and the United States. In addition, organized Greyhound racing — in which Greyhounds race around an oval track chasing an artificial lure (usually a mechanical rabbit) — is a popular sport much like horse racing.

Although not for inexperienced owners, the Greyhound, a quiet and clean breed, also makes an excellent pet. As its dark, bright eyes reveal, the Greyhound is an intelligent, spirited dog.

IBIZAN HOUND

Pictured on the tombs of Egyptian Pharaohs as early as 3000 BC, the rare Ibizan Hound probably descends from ancient Egyptian hunting dogs. These dogs were brought by Phoenician or Libyan merchant vessels to Ibiza, an island off the coast of Spain and from which the dog's English name is derived. The Ibizan people primarily used the dog to hunt rabbits and other game. They greatly valued the dog and carefully culled all litters, keeping only the purest pups. Eventually, the dog became popular on the Spanish mainland and throughout Europe. In 1956, the breed arrived in the United States; it was recognized by the American Kennel Club in 1979.

Resembling a Greyhound, the graceful and athletic Ibizan Hound has a streamlined body with a level back, and long, slender tail. It also has a long neck, and a long, narrow head with large, upright ears. Its nose is a distinctive pink, and its relatively small eyes are amber colored. It usually stands no more than 25 inches and has a light weight of 42 to 50 pounds.

Most Ibizans are short haired with silky coats, but there is also a long-haired breed that has a thick, more wiry coat. Coat colors are red, white, tawny (lion) or a combination of these. The solid colors are rare, and hence the most desirable.

The Ibizan is a friendly dog which adapts well to family life. Due to its coursing heritage, it is alert and farsighted and loves to run. It hates to be caged or confined, and consequently does very poorly in kennels. The Ibizan enjoys the company of people and other dogs, but, like the true hound it is, shows little respect for cats and other small animals.

With their long necks and streamlined bodies, the Greyhound *(below)* **and the Ibizan Hound** *(right)* **are built for speed.**

GROOMING

The proper care of the coat is of great importance, since the beauty of the animal in so many breeds is dependent on the condition of its hair. In healthy animals if the hair is given proper attention it is bright, glossy, soft, and full of tone, but if neglected or improperly cared for, it becomes dull, harsh and brittle.

Smooth-coated dogs can be efficiently cleaned by brushing and combing. For this purpose an ordinary hairbrush will suffice. The hair should first be stirred up with a vigorous brushing and finished by smoothing it in the direction it should naturally lie by alternate strokes of the brush and the hand.

For wire-haired dogs a stiff brush with long, hard bristles is best. The hair can be thoroughly cleaned by haphazard strokes of the brush in all directions. Brushing the coat in the ordinary way will soften the hair and make it lie smooth, a undesirable condition in dogs of this type. After a thorough brushing the coat can be given a hand massage, which will rough up the hair.

There are two types of long-haired coats, differing only in the presence of the undercoat. Setters and Spaniels have one long outercoat, while Collies, Chows and Pomeranians have an additional short, woolly undergrowth. Long-haired dogs must be first combed to remove the snarls, the dead undercoat and the loose hair. The coat should then be thoroughly brushed with a heavy stiff-bristled brush and finished with a light, soft brush.

Right: **Brushing is important for all dogs, even short-haired ones like Dachshunds** *(below)* **and Bulldogs** *(far right).*

When a ruff is desired it can be worked up with the hand or brush last.

In addition to frequent brushing, the dog requires an occasional bath to keep its coat clean and looking its best. The average house dog should be washed approximately once a month, using any good mild soap. The actions of the individual dog determine, to a great extent, the frequency of the bath. Some animals are naturally clean and take great pride in keeping their coats in fine condition, while others delight in rolling in all the dirt to be found. However, too frequent bathing is more detrimental to the coat than not enough because it can irritate the skin and cause eczema.

Very thin or sick dogs should not be bathed, nor should puppies before they are at least four months old. Puppies are usually frightened during their first bath and will try to get away. If badly handled, they will always fight their bath, hence great care must be spent in getting them used to the procedure. The first bath should be made as short as possible, both because of the dog's fear and the danger of contracting a cold.

To bathe a dog, it should be placed in a dry tub and accustomed to it. The dog's face and feet can be washed first, with water from a basin. As the dog becomes used to the water, more can be poured into the tub, little by little, until there is a sufficient amount for the bath. The hair of the body can be saturated by scooping the water up by the hand. Dogs that like the bath may be induced to lie in the water, or it can be poured over them with a dipper. After the hair is saturated, the soap can be applied, the lather being thoroughly worked through the hair to the skin to dislodge all of the dirt. The soap is then washed out and the dog thoroughly rinsed with clear water. The first water should be hot and the rinsing water cooled as much as the dog can stand.

The thoroughness with which the dog need be dried will depend on the kind of animal it is and the condition of the weather. The small toys must be absolutely dry, while in the large, strong dogs only the bulk of the water need be removed. In winter, drying is more important than in summer. To dry your dog, the hair is first squeezed with the hands until all of the water possible has been removed and then towels are used to absorb the remainder of the moisture.

Chows *(below)* **and Collies** *(right)* **need frequent brushings to keep their luxurious coats looking clean and beautiful.**

IRISH SETTER

The Irish Setter is considered by some to be one of the most beautiful dogs in the world. In addition to its outstanding mahogany-red coat, the dog is known for its elegant build and graceful movements. The stunningly handsome Irish Setter truly looks like an aristocrat of dogs.

Although its exact origin is unknown, the Irish Setter was well established in Ireland by the early 1800s. Its lineage probably traces back to a medieval hunting dog, the Setting Spaniel, which was trained to find birds and then to set (crouch or lie down) so that a net could be thrown over the birds and dog. The Irish Setter's ancestry probably includes the English and Gordon Setters, and some Pointers as well.

In Ireland, the Irish Setter was highly regarded as a hunting dog and a gundog. By 1880, the dog's popularity as a hunter's companion had spread well outside of Ireland. As more people began to use the dog on hunts, however, the Irish Setter began to acquire a reputation for being 'unsteady' in the field. This reputation was basically unfair because what most hunters didn't realize was that the Irish Setter needs more training and firmer handling than most gundogs. The reputation stuck, however, and today the Irish Setter is used as a sporting dog to hunt birds only.

In the nineteenth century, all Irish Setters were red with white markings on the forehead, chest and feet. Over time, however, the white markings have largely disappeared, and the solid red color has become the most common, and certainly the most preferred for shows in the United States and Canada. In Ireland, both solid reds and the red and white dogs are still exhibited.

Lighter and of a rangier build than other Setters, the Irish Setter has a long-legged, lithe and muscular body. Its head is lean and long, with a chiseled muzzle, and it has almond-shaped eyes set far apart. Its flat and silky coat is short on the head, forelegs, and ear tips, and longer and feathered on the backs of the legs, the underparts, the tail and between the toes. Although long in body, the Irish Setter's build looks substantial and, indeed, its stamina is almost limitless. This stamina, coupled with the dog's swiftness, made the Irish Setter physically well suited to its old role of hunting dog.

Even today, the Irish Setter needs an enormous amount of exercise if it is to be a good pet. Without this exercise, the lively and energetic Irish Setter can be difficult to manage. The lively and energetic Irish Setter is also highly intelligent, however, and therefore highly trainable. In addition to being loving, good-tempered, and demonstrative, the Irish Setter is a true clown with an almost rollicking personality. The Irish Setter is also the nicest thief you'll ever meet — it absolutely loves to find treasures to bring home to its owner.

Right: **Its red, glossy coat enhances the Irish Setter's aristocratic bearing.** *Below:* **This energetic dog requires a lot of activity.**

IRISH TERRIER

Nicknamed 'the daredevil,' the Irish Terrier is an incredibly courageous dog that served as sentinel and was used to carry messages on the battlefield during World War I and World War II. Although its life today is generally much more sedate, the Irish Terrier still retains a bold and fearless spirit, and is considered one of the best guard dogs in the world.

Although its exact origins are unknown, the Irish Terrier is not indigenous to Ireland. It is, however, one of the oldest breeds of terriers, and was used in Ireland as a ratter and to hunt and retrieve game. First exhibited in England in 1870, the Irish Terrier achieved much popularity in Britain, and, in later years, in North America. The dog was especially popular in Boston, Massachusetts, where it was the beloved pet of many Irish immigrants.

Built like a Fox Terrier, the Irish Terrier has much racier lines than other terriers. It is also longer bodied and of lighter weight than most dogs its height (approximately 18 inches tall). The angular profile of the Irish Terrier shows off a deep, muscular chest, a level, strong back, and straight, well-boned legs. It also shows a long, rectangular-shaped head (with a short beard), and a flat skull that is relatively narrow between the dog's button ears. The Irish Terrier's eyes are small and dark, and its docked tail is carried erect.

The short coat of the Irish Terrier is dense and wiry, and lies flat against the body. Some Irish Terriers have curly or kinky coats but neither is acceptable for show purposes. The color of the coat is red, red-wheaten, or golden red. Occasionally, an Irish Terrier will have a small, white patch on its chest, but again, this is not permissible in shows.

Today, when not being used as a guard dog, the Irish Terrier is cherished as a family pet. Extremely loyal and protective, the Irish Terrier will defend its loved ones against any danger. It is also exceptionally devoted to its owners and has been known to track them down over incredible distances. Although gentle with the people it knows, the Irish Terrier has a strong sense of property and a deserved reputation as a fighter. A wise owner will give the Irish Terrier lots of exercise and keep it away from other animals, especially from males.

These pages: **Speed and endurance are among the Irish Terrier's qualities — as are loyalty, devotion and pluck.**

ITALIAN GREYHOUND

This exquisite and elegant little dog is believed to have originated more than 2000 years ago in the Mediterranean basin. The remains of a similar dog were found in an Egyptian tomb of 6000 years ago, and dogs resembling the present-day Greyhound are depicted on the tombs of the pharaohs. Its image is also on the early decorative arts of Greece and Turkey, and small Greyhound skeletons have been discovered by archaeologists digging in those countries.

The Phoenicians brought the toy-sized Greyhound (as well as the standard-sized Greyhound) to Italy, where it was adored by Roman matrons. One historian has suggested the sign *Cave Canem* (beware of the dog) on old Roman villas refers not to the giant, chained Mastiff, but rather to the tiny Italian Greyhound that the unwarned visitor might trample underfoot.

By the Middle Ages the breed had spread throughout Southern Europe, and it reached a peak of popularity with the Italians of the sixteenth century, resulting in its being called the Italian Greyhound. During the Renaissance, it became known in Northern Europe as well, and artists such as Giotto, Carpaccio, Memling, Van der Weyden, Gerard David, Hieronymus Bosch, and others captured the naturally graceful posture, awake or asleep, of the small dog.

The Italian Greyhound was a favorite of royalty, including the consorts of James I and James II of England, Anne of Denmark and Mary Beatrice d'Este of Modena; Francis I of France; Frederick the Great of Prussia; Catherine the Great of Russia; and Queen Victoria, who liked Italian Greyhounds so well she bred them in her kennels. Frederick the Great took his Italian Greyhound with him wherever he went, and once, during the Seven Years' War, the tide of battle having suddenly turned for the worse, the king was forced to hide under a bridge. The little dog nestled in his arms kept silent as the troops thundered overhead. Had he barked, Frederick would have been discovered and doubtless killed. When his tiny companion died, the king buried him with his own hands in the palace garden in Berlin.

An African tribal ruler, taken by the toy dog's high-stepping gait, which has been compared to the prancing of a hackney pony, offered two hundred head of cattle for one of these dainty dogs. The French poet and statesman Alphonse de Lamartine immortalized the Italian Greyhound in his poems.

In recent years the breed has enjoyed great popularity, competing successfully in dog shows and obedience trials and winning a number of Best-in-Show awards. Weighing between six and 10 pounds and measuring 12 to 15 inches tall, the Italian Greyhound is a miniature Greyhound, developed by breeding only the smallest specimens of the Greyhound, and thus is a pure breed. Its head is narrow and long, with small, folded ears, except when alerted, and large, expressive eyes. A gracefully arched neck flows into long, sloping shoulders. Its body is of medium length, with lean muscles, set on long, delicate legs, with well-arched toes. The tail, carried low, is tapered and covered with fine hair. The short, silky coat may be fawn, red, mouse, blue, cream or white, with white paws and chest permitted. The official standard for the Italian Greyhound was established in Italy.

Whether the Italian Greyhound was bred to be a hunting dog or a house pet is unknown. It can reach speeds of about 40 miles an hour, and therefore can catch rabbits on the run, and it loves flushing partridge and other birds from the underbrush. But its ideal role would seem to be as a pampered pet. It is extremely affectionate and sensitive and shivers from emotion, not the cold, but a loving caress will usually quiet the agitation. This playful, vivacious, and charming dog is meant to be admired and adored and provided with a pillow by the fire, along with frequent promenades on a leash. And don't count on it sounding the alarm in the event of a nighttime prowler; this tiny greyhound would probably run, without a sound, and jump under the covers with you, if it wasn't already there.

Facing page: **A trio of speedsters — the Italian Greyhound is the smallest of the three, the Greyhound the largest. The Whippet ranks in the middle.**
Right: **The pint-sized Japanese Chin.**

JAPANESE CHIN

This lively, high stepping little dog probably originated in China, since similar dogs are depicted on ancient Chinese temples, pottery and embroidery dating back several centuries before Christ. But it was the Japanese who developed the toy dog after a pair was given by the Emperor of China to the Emperor of Japan in the eighth century BC, and for more than 1000 years he became the favorite of Japanese emperors. In fact, one emperor decreed all Japanese Spaniels (In 1977 the AKC officially changed their name to Japanese Chin) were to be worshipped, and some small dogs were kept in cages like birds. It was also the custom to carry them in the loose sleeves of their kimonos.

For years these pampered pets were owned only by members of the nobility and now and then presented to distinguished foreigners who had performed some great service for Japan. Then in 1853 Commodore Matthew Calbraith Perry, ordered to Japan by President Millard Fillmore to induce the government to establish diplomatic relations with the US, succeeded in his mission and opened the country's trade to the world. Perry was given some Japanese Spaniels and he gave two to Queen Victoria, which made the breed known in England. Queen Alexandra, in turn, took an interest in the little dogs, and, to emphasize Britain's neutrality during the Russo-Japanese War, she had her picture taken with a Russian Wolfhound (Borzoi) at her right side and a Japanese Spaniel under her left arm.

After Perry's voyage, demand for the dogs increased in America, as well as in England, and dognapping became rife in Japan. Ships took on contingents of dogs and spread them all over the world, but sadly they did not live long. World War I entirely cut off the supply of new dogs from Japan, and American breeders had to work with the dogs they already owned.

Fickle is fashion and when the Pekingese appeared on the scene in 1860 interest in the Japanese Spaniel decreased, although the breed was recognized by the AKC in 1888. Even Japanese fanciers turned their attention to other dogs. But today the Chin is alive and increasing in Europe and America.

Production of miniature species became an art in Japan and included plants along with dogs. Unfortunately, emphasizing the diminutive size of the dogs had a negative effect on their health and fertility, and Chins are still more susceptible to distemper than most dogs.

The Chin looks like a tall, slim cousin of the Pekingese, with a silkier coat, that is usually black and white, but may also be red, sable, brindle, lemon or orange and white. Its profuse coat gives a very showy appearance. The Chin weighs between four and nine pounds and measures about 10 inches at the shoulders. White must show in the inner corner of the Japanese Chin's large, dark, prominent, and widely set eyes, for this gives the dog its characteristic quizzical look. Another trait of this dainty dog is its amusing way of twirling around, almost as if dancing.

KEESHOND

The worldwide political unrest preceding the French Revolution led to the Keeshond (pronounced Kayshond) coming to prominence. Holland in the late eighteenth century was divided into two rival camps, the *Prinsgezinden*, or partisans of the Prince of Orange, and the *Patriotten*, or Patriots. The leader of the Patriots, Cornelius 'Kees' de Gyselaer, owned a little spitz dog, which became known as 'the dog of Kees' or 'Keeshond.' He chose this dog as the symbol of the Patriots, while the Royalists had the Pug as their mascot. The political pictures and cartoons of the time include the Keeshond, whose spirit the rebels believed typified their own.

When the House of Orange was restored to power, the Keeshond disappeared from cities, but could still be found in the countryside and on the waterways. Before becoming politicized, the breed had served as a guard dog and pet for uncountable years on the rijnaken, or barges, that plied the canals, and as a result was also called 'the Dutch Barge Dog.'

The ancestors of the Keeshond undoubtedly came from the Arctic and were responsible also for its cousins — the Samoyed, the Siberian Husky, the Norwegian Elkhound, the Finnish Spitz, the Pomeranian and others. Resembling most the Pomeranian, the Keeshond is thought by some experts to have been selectively bred to produce that tiny canine. Old paintings and drawings show how little the Keeshond has changed over the centuries. In a drawing done in 1794 the children and Keeshond of a *bürgermeister* mourn beside his tomb. Other examples of Keeshonden are found in the paintings of Jan Steen, a well known Dutch artist.

Until 1920 the Keeshond was in eclipse. Then the Baroness van Hardenbroek, through careful breeding and energetic public relations, revived the breed and re-established the barge dog's popularity. Within 10 years the Dutch Keeshond Club was founded and a standard was accepted for judging the breed, and today the Keeshond is the National Dog of Holland. Mrs Wingfield-Digby introduced some specimens to England in 1925 and the breed was registered by the American Kennel Club in 1930.

This handsome dog has a compact body, alert carriage and foxy face, with an intelligent expression. It has small pointed ears, a large ruff and luxurious wolf grey coat, with a feathered tail curled over its back. The Keeshond is 17 to 18 inches tall and wears trousers of thick fur on its hind legs and gently drawn spectacles adorn its eyes. All members of the spitz family are friendly, affectionate, inclined to be noisy and require frequent brushing. They are very attached to their families but may ignore strangers or bark sharply at them.

KOMONDOR

The Komondor is sometimes described as looking like a walking floor mop. Its heavy, shaggy, white coat is so woolly in texture that it becomes matted and corded if uncombed. Today the coat is usually kept well groomed, but over a 1000 years ago the mop effect was carefully cultivated.

Brought to Europe in the ninth century by the Magyars when they invaded Hungary, the Komondor was used to protect sheep on the mountainsides of Hungary. The Komondor was responsible for driving wolves, foxes and bears from the pasture, as well as prowlers from its master's estate. The Hungarian shepherds deliberately let the coat become tangled and corded because it provided the dog with excellent protection from the fangs of the predators it was driving away.

The Komondor's great size (up to 95 pounds), robustness, and thick coat also help it withstand all kinds of harsh and inclement weather. Its coat is always white, unless the dog is kept in the city and unbathed; then the coat turns a dirty grey. Not surprisingly, bathing the Komondor is a chore, requiring long hours of drying time.

The Komondor — like most humans — needs a purpose in life; it likes to work and is still well suited for being an excellent watchdog. It is, in fact, a guard dog by nature, and is very aggressive towards strangers and other dogs. Although extremely powerful and headstrong, the Komondor is also a very loyal dog, devoted to, and playful with, its human family.

The Komondor is often thought of as a country dog because it needs a lot of exercise, and some say the dog also needs obedience training. Basically, the Komondor is an ideal dog for those who desire a dog with an unusual appearance and who don't mind a grooming challenge.

Below: **The Komondor at work guarding sheep.** *Right:* **The Komondor is covered with a heavy coat of cords that feel like felt.**

LABRADOR RETRIEVER

Considered one of the very best all-round dogs in the world, the Labrador Retriever has excelled as a field dog, a household pet, a show dog and a guide dog. Its steadfast, affectionate, and gentle nature makes it one of the most esteemed and ideal family dogs in existence.

Originally imported from Newfoundland (and not Labrador, Canada), the Labrador Retriever was developed in England and made popular by the Earl of Malmesbury. The Earl gave the dog its Labrador name and was one of the first to recognize the dog's wonderful talents and characteristics. Although originally trained to flush and retrieve game, the Labrador later demonstrated an even more valuable skill: During wartime, the Labrador saved many lives by using its strong nose to detect mines buried at considerable depths.

Physically, the Labrador Retriever is a largish dog with two outstanding characteristics: its coat and its tail. The coat — which is usually black, but also yellow or chocolate — is short, thick and water-resistant. Unlike that of the Golden Retriever, the Labrador's coat has no waves and no feathering. The tail is long, unusually thick at the base, and tapers towards the tip.

The Labrador has a wonderfully large head with a powerful neck, and a strong build composed of a wide chest, a short back and muscular hindquarters. Unlike many dogs with eyes that come in only one or two colors, its eyes may be brown, hazel, yellow or black.

The sporting Labrador is a very obedient dog, extremely alert and quick to learn. For this reason, the Labrador is popular in the show ring and is frequently used as a guide dog. No matter what its role, however, the fairly hardy Labrador loves to work and is especially eager to exercise. As is true for the Golden Retriever, the ideal Labrador workout should include occasional swims.

The very loving Labrador should always be treated in kind, for this big-hearted dog is keenly sensitive and suffers badly under any kind of bullying. The Lab's vivacious personality, combined with its willingness to please, has made it one of the most popular dogs in both the United States and England.

A 'people dog,' the Labrador Retriever *(these pages)* **is readily trained because of its background as a hunting dog. The close relationship between the hunter and his dog necessitates a dog that instantly understands what its master wants.**

LHASA APSO

The origins of the Lhasa Apso seem as shrouded in mist as the Himalayan mountains. It is believed to be one of the world's most ancient dogs, perhaps dating back to 800 BC, and may have developed from the two other Tibetan breeds in the AKC Non-Sporting Group, the Tibetan Spaniel and the Tibetan Terrier.

Its name comes from the sacred city of Lhasa and Apso may derive from the Tibetan word *rapso*, meaning 'goatlike,' given his thick, golden coat, but more likely it is a slightly changed form of the Abso in his Tibetan nickname *Abso Seng Kye*, signifying 'Bark Lion Sentinel Dog.'

Danger lurked from without and within long ago in royal houses and monasteries in the lofty mountains of Tibet, and as protection nobles and lamas kept a large Mastiff chained to a post beside the outer door and at least one small Lhasa Apso inside. The latter is especially well suited to guard duty owing to his keen sense of hearing, intelligence and innate ability to distinguish friend from foe. In addition to acting as a watch dog, this woolly little canine was a participant in religious ceremonies, where, splendidly seated on a silken cushion and surrounded by solemn ritual, he was considered, according to legend, a reincarnated lama who had not yet ascended to Paradise.

For centuries the Lhasa Apso existed almost exclusively in Tibet, a country which has always been difficult to reach and not especially welcoming to foreigners. Only lamas, dignitaries and high-ranking military officers were allowed to own Lhasas. They were never sold, since Buddhism forbids selling living things, but were given as a mark of great esteem. A few males were bestowed upon honored Chinese guests, but no females, thus insuring that future production of the breed remained in Tibetan hands. Lhasas arrived in Britain and North America in the 1920s as presents from the Dalai Lama. Known as good luck dogs, they were called Talisman Dogs or Lhasa Terriers until 1934 in England. The AKC moved them from the Terrier to the Non-Sporting Group in 1955. Among those who raised Lhasa Apsos was Tenzing Norkay, the Sherpa guide who accompanied Sir Edmund Hillary to the top of Mount Everest.

The little Lhasa's body is covered with a long, flowing coat which hides its face and body. Sometimes, at maturity, the coat is so long that it reaches the ground. The silky hair is especially abundant on the Lhasa's hanging ears, its neck, and its plumed tail (which it carries high over its back). The hair covering the face forms a full beard and whiskers. Peeking through the hair are two dark brown eyes and a black nose. The Tibetans — and many owners today — prefer their Lhasas to have lion-like coloring, but the coats vary widely in color, including gold, sand, honey, slate, smoke, black, white or brown. Dark tips on the ears and beard are highly regarded.

Despite its toy dog appearance, the Lhasa is a very proud, hardy and fearless dog. It may look cuddly, but its boldness and oftentimes quick temper does not make it the best lapdog or children's pet. The Lhasa is reserved with strangers, but affectionate with owners. It shows special affection for the owner who keeps its long, luxuriant coat in glorious condition. The Lhasa loves to play and greatly enjoys a good romp in the snow or other similar vigorous exercise. The Lhasa is reputed to be able to sense oncoming avalanches, and its fur is used to make beautiful blankets and sweaters.

MINIATURE BULL TERRIER

The Miniature Bull Terrier is a smaller-sized version of the Bull Terrier, created by crossing the smallest Bull Terriers born over a period of time. *(See Bull Terrier.)* It may weigh up to 20 pounds and be no more than 14 inches tall. Because Miniatures are difficult to breed, their numbers are few. The Miniature Bull Terrier was recognized by the British Kennel Club in 1943 and is in the American Kennel Club's Miscellaneous Class.

Right: **The gay and assertive Lhasa Apso is sometimes wary of strangers.** ***Facing page:*** **A Miniature Schnauzer and her puppy.**

MINIATURE SCHNAUZER TERRIER

Most popular of all the terriers, the Miniature Schnauzer is a high-spirited little dog with a very friendly disposition. Hardy and handsome, the intelligent Miniature Schnauzer adapts well to city or country life and makes an ideal pet.

Unlike all other terriers, the Miniature Schnauzer does not trace back to the British Isles, but originated in Germany about 1900. Developed by mating a Standard Schnauzer with an Affenpinscher, the new breed was used on farms and around stables as a ratter. By the 1920s, the Miniature Schnauzer had arrived in England and in the United States. An American Miniature Schnauzer Club was founded in 1933.

Standing only 12 to 14 inches tall, the Miniature Schnauzer is the smallest member of the three-member Schnauzer family. (The other two members are the Standard Schnauzer and the Giant Schnauzer.) Greatly resembling the Standard Schnauzer, the Miniature has a short, deep body with straight forelegs and angular hindquarters. Its head is strong and rectangular, and includes a strong muzzle, a thick, shaggy beard, and long, bushy eyebrows. The Miniature's dark eyes are small and deep set, and its ears are pointed. The docked, high-set Miniature tail is carried erect.

Like the other members of its family, the Miniature Schnauzer has a double coat consisting of a hard, wiry outercoat and close undercoat. Most Miniature Schnauzer coats are clipped on the top, and the beard and eyebrows are trimmed. The color of the coat can be black, black and silver or pepper and salt, but the latter variety requires a great deal of maintenance. Although less aggressive than many terriers, the Miniature Schnauzer is still courageous and alert, and thus makes a wonderful watchdog. The Miniature is also a friendly and companionable dog, well-suited for elderly people and children. Active in nature, the Miniature needs some sort of daily exercise, but having received that, the dog is content to stay at home.

NORWEGIAN ELKHOUND

The Norwegian Elkhound dates back to the days of the Vikings, over 6000 years ago. Although used as an all-purpose hunter, shepherd, guard and companion dog, the Norwegian Elkhound's main original function was to hunt elk. The Elkhound's tracking ability is excellent, with hunters today claiming the dog can scent an elk up to three miles away. When not hunting elk, the Norwegian Elkhound was often used for hunting bears or wolves, protecting the village herds from attack by these animals or for pulling sleds.

In the early twentieth century, the Elkhound was brought to the United States. Misunderstanding the Scandinavian word for dog, *hund*, to mean hound, Americans called the dog the Norwegian Elkhound. The mistake was soon discovered, of course, but because the dog is such a highly competent hunter of elk, the Elkhound name stuck. The name has caused some confusion because the Elkhound bears absolutely no resemblance to any other breed in the hound group.

Physically, the Norwegian Elkhound looks like a cross between a German Shepherd and a northern sled dog. Its smooth coat is of black-tipped grey hair which sheds heavily, just like a German Shepherd's. Its erect, pointed ears are also like a Shepherd's. The rest of the Elkhound body is very compact, almost to the point of forming a square, and more closely resembles a northern sled dog. Characteristics distinguishing the dog from both the Shepherd and the sled dog are tightly closed lips, small feet and a full, natural tail that curls high over the back.

One common role for the Norwegian Elkhound today is as a watchdog. In addition to being a very bold dog, the Elkhound has a high-pitched, piercing bark which is perfect for scaring intruders away. The Elkhound is also a very loyal dog, and exceptionally protective of its family. If being considered as a family pet, however, the Elkhound should receive some training at an early age because it is a very stubborn dog with a strong, willful nature. Called by some a classic hardhead, the Elkhound needs to understand who is the leader of the pack.

Below: **The Norwegian Elkhound has recently enjoyed a surge of popularity in the United States.** *Right:* **A fluffy Elkhound puppy.**

NORWICH TERRIER

The Norwich Terrier is probably the only breed with an almost identical twin—the Norfolk Terrier. In fact, the Norwich Terrier and the Norfolk Terrier are so alike that until 1964 they were considered the same dog! There is one difference between them, however: The Norwich's ears stand straight up, while the Norfolk's ears bend forward. The English Kennel Club recognized this difference in 1964; the American Kennel Club, in 1978.

Developed in 1880 in England, the Norwich Terrier was primarily bred as a hunting dog in the urban communities of Cambridge, Market Harborough and Norwich. The Norwich proved to be an excellent dog for chasing foxes out of holes, and it was equally adept at catching rabbits and rats. Cambridge students particularly enjoyed the hunting skills of the Norwich, and later, when the dog arrived in America, it was favored by American hunting clubs for its rabbit-catching abilities.

This short-legged, short-tailed terrier has a stocky build and a harsh, wiry, short double coat. The outercoat is straight and wiry, and the undercoat very thick. The hair is longer on the head than on the rest of the body, giving a suggestion of a mane around the neck and chest. There is also enough hair on the face to form slight whiskers and eyebrows. The dense, rough coat usually comes in the colors of red, reddish brown, wheaten, black and tan, grey or brindle.

The small, rugged Norwich almost always shows a lot of spunk and especially high spirits. It is very active indoors and out, often exhibiting a wanderlust for adventure. Sometimes this adventure seems to be digging to China (the Norwich *loves* to dig), and sometimes it's getting involved in a good fight.

Although stubborn and a little too quick-tempered for small children, the Norwich Terrier is an affectionate and personable dog that adapts well to any environment or person. A family looking for a quiet, docile dog, however, might not adapt well to the Norwich. Only for the family that can appreciate a feisty, hard-headed, pocket-sized dynamo is the Norwich the perfect choice.

These pages: **The diminutive (11 to 12 pounds) Norwich Terrier has a hardy constitution, and is feisty but never quarrelsome.**

OLD ENGLISH SHEEPDOG

The Old English Sheepdog is such a cuddly, loveable looking dog that it has probably been painted in more pictures and written about in more books than any other breed. A 1771 painting by Gainsborough of the Duke of Buccleuch shows the nobleman with his arms around the neck of an Old English Sheepdog. This is the first known picture of the breed. Philip Reinagle (1749 – 1833), celebrated canine artist, did one of his finest paintings of the Old English Sheepdog. Its most famous role, perhaps, is as the beloved *Nana* in JM Barrie's *Peter Pan*.

Its most distinctive characteristic is a shaggy, double coat which covers its eyes and gives its big head a very rounded appearance. The coat is so thick that, at one time, combings from the coat were used to make wool garments in England. Although the coat does not totally obscure the dog's vision, it probably contributes to the Old English Sheepdog's gait, which many say resembles that of a slow, shuffling bear. The coat is usually white with a liberal amount of black or grey, and often there are distinct white markings around the dog's dark eyes.

In addition to the dense, bushy coat, the Old English Sheepdog has a big, black nose, medium-sized hanging ears which it carries flat against its head, and, for its size, remarkably small, round feet. The Old English Sheepdog usually has a bobtail, which is to say almost no tail at all because most of it is removed soon after birth. Even when not absent or docked, the tail is still very short.

It is generally thought the Old English Sheepdog is the result of a crossing of several different herding dogs by farmers in the west of England, in the counties of Devon, Somerset and the Duchy of Cornwall, and those breeds mentioned as possible ancestors or relatives include the Scotch Bearded Collie, the Russian Owtchar, the Hungarian Puli, the French Briard and the Italian Bergamasco. By the mid nineteenth century, the Old English Sheepdog was a familiar sight in the English countryside, and was used throughout Europe to drive sheep and cattle to market.

The hardworking English Sheepdog makes a fine pet and a good companion. Although a slow learner, it is very affectionate, sensible and extremely devoted to the family. In fact, like *Peter Pan's Nana*, the Old English Sheepdog usually feels it is a member of the family. Incredibly exuberant when young, the Old English Sheepdog slows down and becomes more docile as it grows older. Young or old, however, the dog is happiest in a large home with a large yard with owners who give it plenty of exercise. Ideal owners should also give plenty of time to grooming the big dog's shaggy coat — at least two hours a week to keep the dog in peak condition.

Below: **Hidden beneath this shaggy mop of hair are two dark eyes.**
Right: **The loveable Old English Sheepdog.**

PEKINGESE

A very old breed, the Pekingese is portrayed in the art and sculpture of the ancient Chinese dynasties. The Pekingese is the sacred dog of the temple, and it was once so carefully guarded that its theft was punishable by death. The breed was first brought to England in 1869 by Admiral Lord John Hay, who found a few dogs in the Garden of the Summer Palace, where they had doubtless been left when the court fled the approaching forces.

The Pekingese has the short muzzle, full eyes, dome head and pompon tail of all toy spaniels, but it surpasses all in its elaborate ruff on the chest and long feathering on its sides, thighs and forelegs. The Peke weighs 18 pounds or less, the smaller the better. Though small, the Peke is rugged and strong, often exhibiting a boldness that belies its size. This dog chooses its friends and has been known to have a temper.

POMERANIAN

With its bushy tail curled over its back, the diminutive Pomeranian bears a striking resemblance to the Samoyed, and it is likely that the smaller dog is descended from the larger breed. As a result of selective breeding, many Pomeranians weigh less than five pounds. These tiny creatures have a deep, soft fluffy undercoat and a plentiful overcoat of long, straight glossy hair, which is especially full on the throat, chest and hindquarters. The coat comes in many colors, including black, white, blue, brown, sable, red, orange and fawn. Like most toy dogs, the Pom has a round head. Its nose and ears are pointed, the legs straight and delicate, and its walk is light and perky.

Long a popular pet in England and the United States, the Pomeranian is a bright, active and affectionate dog. It is, however, somewhat timid and nervous and can be snappy around strangers.

Below: **The Pekingese's expression conveys courage and self-esteem.**
Right: **The Pomeranian, another popular toy, is active but docile.**

POODLE

A symbol of fashionable elegance, the Poodle is an elegant-looking dog with a distinctive coat of thick, close curls. Highly intelligent and very popular, the Poodle has a served in a variety of functions, including a water retriever, a performer, and even a truffle hunter. The Poodle uses its scent to locate the edible fungus and then digs it up.

The word poodle comes from the German word *puddel,* which means 'to puddle or splash.' The Poodle probably originated in Germany and was developed as a water retriever. Portions of its coat were originally shaved (or clipped) in order to facilitate the Poodle's swimming ability as a retriever. Only much later did the trims come to be equated with style and elegance. In Russia, large, and usually black, Standard Poodles were often used to pull milk carts. The Poodle achieved its greatest popularity in France, where it was eventually chosen as the national dog. Today, the Poodle's association with France is so strong that some people refer to the dog as the French Poodle.

Just when the Poodle emerged is not known, but bas-reliefs dating from the first century, found on Mediterranean shores, portray him, clipped to resemble the lion, very much as he is today. A favorite subject of artists, the Poodle probably appears in more works of art than any other dog. Botticelli (1445 – 1510) was one of the first well-known painters to paint him. Dürer (1471 – 1528) made the breed more widely recognized with his drawings. Pinturicchio, the Italian artist, and de Vos, the Flemish artist, painted him about the same time. He is also seen in works by Rembrandt (1606 – 1669). In the eighteenth century the Poodle became the principal pet dog of Spain and was painted by Goya. From the seventeenth century on the Poodle became known as a prestigious pet and ladies' dog. Marie Antoinette had a pampered Toy Poodle.

The Poodle comes in three varieties, each differing only in size: The Standard Poodle, the oldest and largest variety, is at least 15 inches; the Miniature Poodle, developed by the French as a companion for the Standard, is between 10 and 15 inches high; and the Toy Poodle is 10 inches or less. The Standard and Miniature Poodles are considered nonsporting dogs by the American Kennel Club, and the Toy Poodle is placed in the Toy category.

All Poodles, regardless of size, have the same dense, wiry coat which can be clipped in several traditional styles. Poodle pups one year or less are usually given the puppy clip which keeps the coat long except for a shaven face, throat, feet, and tail (with a pompon at the end). Adult Poodles usually sport the Continental or English Saddle clip. The Continental requires that the Poodle's hindquarters, face, throat, feet, legs and tail be shaved, leaving bracelets on the hind legs, puffs on the forelegs, and a pompon on the tail. The English Saddle clip leaves the hindquarters covered with a short blanket of hair except for curved shaved areas on the flanks, and two shaved bands on each hind leg. The face, throat, feet, forelegs, and tail are shaved, leaving puffs on the forelegs and, again, a pompon on the tail. If the coat of the Poodle is not clipped or shaven, the hair grows into ropelike cords, and the Poodle is then called a Corded Poodle.

Clip or no clip, all Poodles have well-proportioned bodies and proud carriages. Their square build includes a short back, a deep chest, broad, muscular loins, and straight, parallel forelegs. The head is moderately round, and the ears hang. The Poodle's double coat consists of a woolly undercoat and a dense, wiry topcoat. Poodles come in any solid color.

Loyal, gentle, and very responsive, the Poodle, if well-bred, makes an excellent pet. The Poodle is a good dog for apartment families, although some Toys are too excitable to be around children. The active Poodle needs daily exercise, and with its springy gait, can make a fun jogging partner.

These pages: **The Poodle's enduring popularity is due to the breed's winning personality and distinctive looks.**

PORTUGUESE WATER DOG

Some dogs love to swim, but the Portuguese Water Dog was *made* to swim. With its strongly webbed feet and rudder-like tail, the Portuguese Water Dog is an outstanding swimmer, capable of swimming up to five miles an hour and diving to depths of up to 12 feet.

Although the dog's origin is somewhat uncertain, one theory holds that Portuguese Water Dogs are descended from southern Russian sheep dogs. Migrating Russian tribes brought the dogs to northwest Africa in the 700s. From there, Moor invaders carried the dogs to Portugal where they were bred to be water dogs. For centuries fishermen in the Algarve province of Portugal trained the dogs to pull nets and fish from the ocean. The dogs were especially good at diving for escaping fish, catching them in their mouths and bringing them back to boat or shore. The dogs also sometimes served as messengers between boats or ships. In the late twentieth century, the dog arrived in the United States. The breed was recognized by the American Kennel Club in 1983.

Except for its webbed feet, the Portuguese Water Dog looks like the big working dog that it is. It has a strong, nicely proportioned body, with a wide head and a tapering muzzle. Its medium-length tail is undocked and usually freely hanging. If the dog is standing at attention, the tail arches over the body. It has a thick coat, which can be curly or wavy, groomed in either of two styles: The lion clip has the face and hindquarters shaved; the working-retriever clip keeps the hair shortened over the body and slightly longer on the legs and head.

Both clips have the tail shaved to a pompon at the end. The color of the coat is black or brown (like the dog's eyes) or greyish white or varying degrees of white.

The intelligent and calm Portuguese Water Dog makes an excellent family pet. It loves to act the clown, and generally tries to please everyone. Because it is a nonshedder, it is an especially good dog for people allergic to long-haired animals. The Portuguese Water Dog is a very active dog, however, and serious about its exercise. Because it so loves to swim, the ideal owner will not only provide the Portuguese Water Dog with love and affection, but also plenty of opportunities to engage in the sport for which it is so superbly suited.

The strong and powerfully built Portuguese Water Dog (*these pages*) loves to swim. This athletic dog makes a fine companion.

PUG

The largest of the toy-size dogs, the Pug — with its massive head and deeply wrinkled face — is not what one would call a beauty. But what it lacks in looks, it makes up for in personality. Called the jester of toy breeds, the pug is a fun-loving, impish dog that greatly enjoys life.

The Pug originated in China sometime before 400 BC. It was a favorite pet of the Tibetan monks and became popular in Japan. The Pug was introduced to Europe in the sixteenth century by Dutch traders, who discovered the dog during the course of their travels. The breed gained great popularity in the Netherlands after a Pug reportedly warned a prince of approaching Spanish invaders. For this heroic deed, the Pug was adopted as mascot by the Dutch House of Orange. By the late 1700s, the Pug was popular throughout Europe. In later centuries, however, the Pug's popularity began to decline, almost to the point of extinction. Not until the dog was imported to the United States, and sometime after World War II, did the Pug's numbers begin to increase.

Today the Pug is greatly valued as a companion dog, a dog that is friendly, playful and ready to frolic at any time. Loyal, alert and almost always good-humored, the Pug makes an excellent family dog. The Pug just seems to enjoy life, and, although often impulsive and headstrong, it is more often spoiled than disciplined.

The toy Pug has a short, compact body and a broad chest. Its distinguishing feature is a large, round head with a deeply wrinkled face that is partially covered by a black mask. Its muzzle is square and blunt, and its small, soft ears usually fold forward close to the head. Another reason the Pug is so often spoiled are its eyes — large, dark and round, the eyes have such a soft expression that it is difficult to remain angry with a Pug for any length of time. The Pug has a tightly curled tail that lies on either side of its back. A tail with a double curl is considered perfect.

The coat of the Pug is smooth, short and glossy, and comes in the colors of silver, apricot, fawn, and black. Some apricot-colored Pugs have a black line along their back from the top of their skull to the tail. Because the Pug's muzzle, mask and ears are black, apricot or fawn Pugs are preferred in order to show good contrast with the black markings.

Although the little Pug seems an almost ideal pet, it should be noted that it sheds heavily, it can be a picky eater, it needs lots of exercise — more than most toy dogs — and it snores when asleep.

He may never win a beauty contest, but the Pug *(these pages)* **is irresistible in his own way.**

Above: The large, lustrous eyes add to the appeal of these impish Pug puppies.

RHODESIAN RIDGEBACK

Also known as the African Lion Dog, the Rhodesian Ridgeback was developed in South Africa and made popular in Rhodesia. In addition to being one of the few dogs bred to hunt lions, the Rhodesian Ridgeback is the only dog to be distinctively marked by a ridge of raised hair along its back.

The Rhodesian Ridgeback inherited its hunting abilities and its unique ridge from half-wild, prick-eared Hottentot hunting dogs which interbred with European dogs belonging to Boer settlers in Cape Province. In 1876, some of these settlers brought the dog to Rhodesia, where it quickly gained popularity as a big game hunting dog. It was in Rhodesia that the dog acquired its nickname of the African Lion Dog and its real name of Rhodesian Ridgeback. In 1950, the dog was brought from the African veld to the United States, and, in 1955, it was adopted by the American Kennel Club.

The Rhodesian Ridgeback's body is especially well suited for Africa's rugged bush and dramatic changes in temperature. Although not a very big dog, the trim-looking Rhodesian Ridgeback has a strong build, with a broad chest and back, heavily boned forelegs and extremely muscular hindlegs. Its short, hard, glossy coat is perfect for running through the African grasslands and for enduring scorching days or freezing nights. Even the color of its coat — yellow to reddish-brown — helps the Ridgeback by blending nicely with the African countryside.

Although highly intelligent, the Ridgeback is by nature a stubborn dog and could do well with obedience training. The very active Ridgeback also requires plenty of exercise if it is to be truly happy. Outside of the exercise requirement, however, the Ridgeback is a fairly easy dog to keep. This is especially true when it comes to its culinary requirements. No doubt in Africa its diet consisted of more exotic fare, but, in the Western World, the Ridgeback is known to thrive on American dog food, particularly favoring the kibbled varieties.

SAINT BERNARD

Credited with saving more than 2500 lives, the St Bernard breed is famous for rescuing lost travelers in the snow. The St Bernard is also famous for being the only dog associated with having a small cask of reviving spirits hanging from a collar around its neck. Interestingly enough, however, this reputation is unfounded because the St Bernard never traditionally carried casks — or flasks — on rescue missions. Responsibility for creating the image of the St. Bernard as a bearer of alcoholic beverages goes to an English artist, Sir Edwin Landseer, whose painting of a St. Bernard with a small cask hanging from a collar around its neck became quite popular.

Developed in Switzerland, the St Bernard probably descended from large, mastiff-like dogs from Asia introduced to Europe by the Romans. The breed name was coined in the nineteenth century and originated from the dogs' association with a group of monks living in a monastery in the Swiss Alps. The monastery was founded by St Bernard de Menthon in the 1600s and was called the Hospice of St Bernard. It was located near the St Bernard Pass, which was frequently used by travelers crossing the Alps by foot. By the late seventeenth century, the monks were using the dog to help them rescue lost travelers or those who got caught, and sometimes buried, in sudden snowstorms. After locating the hapless traveler with its keen sense of smell, the St Bernard barked loudly to call for help. The St Bernard was also trained to guide travelers over treacherous trails, giving warning of dangerous footing, and to warn of avalanches. The most famous St Bernard is a dog named *Barry* that resided at the Hospice. Before dying in the early 1800s, *Barry* was credited with saving over 40 lives.

At 165 to 180 pounds, the St Bernard is one of the heaviest dogs in existence. Powerfully built, with a large, muscular body, the St Bernard has broad, sloping shoulders, a very broad back and even

As a hunting dog in Africa, the Rhodesian Ridgeback *(above)* developed great endurance and speed. *Right:* The Saint Bernard.

broad feet. The head of the St Bernard can only be described as massive, and includes a short, squarish muzzle, and high-set, sharply drooping ears. All St Bernards have dense, heavy coats, but some are short-haired and others long-haired. The long-haired variety is the result of a cross with the Newfoundland dog in the early nineteenth century. Long-haired or short-haired, St Bernard coats are usually red and white or white and brownish yellow. In addition, some have black or white markings on the chest, feet, noseband, ruff and tip of the tail.

Highly intelligent and with a keen sense of smell, St Bernards continue to be valued as guide dogs for explorers and also as watchdogs. The St Bernard seems to have a need to be with people all its life and therefore makes a good family dog. Because it can be very messy — drooling and shedding — it is probably best kept in the country. If correctly bred and raised, the sweet-dispositioned St Bernard can truly be called a gentle giant.

Though he may look imposing, the Saint Bernard *(below)* has a gentle disposition and enjoys the company of people.

SALUKI

The Saluki is one of — and perhaps the — oldest purebred dog in the world. Dogs resembling the Saluki appear on Sumerian carvings made over 7000 years ago. The ancient Egyptians so revered the Saluki that they called it the 'royal dog of Egypt.' Mummified Salukis have been found buried in the same tombs with Egyptian pharaohs and other people of royal birth. Hundreds of years later the Arabs paid homage to the Saluki, cherishing it as a sacred dog sent by Allah. Even the traditional Moslems exempted the Saluki from their age-old prejudice against dogs.

In the Middle East, the Saluki was used to run down gazelle antelope and other quick-footed game. In Egypt, especially, the Saluki was teamed with hawks for hunting gazelle. The hawk would strike the prey and the Saluki's job was to hold it down until the hunters arrived. In 1840, the Saluki was discovered and brought to England, where instead of being a gazelle dog, it was used to chase hares. By the 1920s, the Saluki had arrived in America and was officially recognized by the American Kennel Club in 1927.

The Saluki's appearance can best be described as regal. Built like a Greyhound, the Saluki has a streamlined body with a well-muscled neck, shoulders and thighs. It has an almost perfect wedge-shaped head with large, lustrous, deep-set eyes and long, silky ears that hang close to the head. The Saluki tail is long and set low. The female Saluki is generally smaller than the male; she is not, however, any less regal in appearance.

Although all Salukis have smooth, soft coats, the long-haired variety has longer and feathered hair on the legs, ears, and tail. The Saluki coat comes in many colors, some of the most common of which are white, cream, pale tan, reddish brown, fawn, black and tan and a combination of colors. The long, silky hair is the Saluki's crowning glory, and it is also found on the underside of the Saluki's tail and on its legs.

A hunter by nature, the Saluki is not especially suited to city life. It does best when given plenty of exercise and room to run. The Saluki is, however, a very good family dog because it seems to need and respond to human attention more than other dogs.

Above and below: **Its large, expressive eyes and long, silky ears give the Saluki a regal appearance.** *Right:* **A cuddly Saluki puppy.**

TRAINING THE DOG

Good manners and clean habits are the chief assets of the pet dog — even though it may possess a wonderful pedigree showing the best of breeding. Training an animal is simply a matter of education, and in the dog the possibilities are far-reaching, for its amiability, intelligence, power of reasoning, and wonderful instincts are coupled with a devotion and faithfulness to its master that prompt it to obey. When these traits are developed the dog is a far more agreeable companion than one that has been allowed to grow up without proper attention to its mental powers. To be well trained the dog does not necessarily need to do tricks. While this is amusing to the owner and sometimes to the animal, it has no bearing on the dog's fitness for the house.

The dog's training should begin while it is still a small puppy, for when it is started early the undertaking is much easier, although progress will be slow. If the dog's education is neglected until it is six or eight months old, the puppy will have acquired many undesirable habits that will be very hard to correct.

The owner must first develop in his dog a feeling of trust and a desire to please. The owner must conduct himself in such a way that the dog will have no cause to fear him. He should never shout at the animal nor scare him. If the dog is naturally timid he must approach him carefully, at the same time talking

Training should start at an early age *(above)*. **Most dogs, like the Bulldog** *below* **and the Poodle** *at right*, **are eager learners.**

encouragingly to him. No attempt should be made to control his actions until the fear is overcome. The dog should not be asked to do anything that will frighten or harm it, nor should the dog be forced to do that which it does not understand. By liberally praising the dog when it does do right and rewarding it with a small treat, a desire to please will be stimulated.

In teaching the dog a task, it must be repeatedly shown what is expected of it until the owner is absolutely sure that it thoroughly understands. Once accomplished, the deed should be frequently repeated until the dog is familiar with it. The dog must not be punished unless the master is certain that the dog knows what is wanted. He should first attempt to coerce the dog by coaxing and talking to it or by bribing it with a dog biscuit. If the dog fails to respond it should be scolded; as a last resort it should be punished. A rolled up newspaper or switch should always be kept for this purpose alone, and the owner should never hit with his hand or with anything else used about the dog, or the dog will always be expecting a licking.

The mind of the dog is capable of much development if the owner is interested enough to stimulate it. The dog can comprehend much from a conversation of simple words such as would be used with a child. In giving commands, however, the same word should always be used for the same act, and the tone of the voice should always convey the spirit of the command. A reprimand should be sufficiently harsh to convey the necessity of obedience.

The dog must be taught to respond to its name, to come when called or to lie down when told. It should learn in what rooms it is forbidden and on what furniture it must not lie. The dog should learn not to beg for food from those at the table. It must be taught not to play with and tear up shoes, or other articles of clothing. The dog must learn not to scratch the rugs or chew the furniture. It must be accustomed to grooming and bathing, and must learn to submit to being handled, to have its mouth opened and examined, to have its ears cleaned and to take medicine.

When on the street, the dog should be controlled by a leash attached to his collar or harness. The dog may want to run in front, and while this is all right at times, it should be taught to heel. This is not a difficult lesson, but is more easily taught older dogs than puppies, for there is some danger of breaking their spirit by being too strict at an early age. Puppies are restless creatures with an inquisitiveness which leads them everywhere, and this, to a certain extent, should be encouraged. When teaching the dog to heel, the owner should shorten the leash as much as possible. If the dog tries to go in front of him as he starts to walk, the animal should be pulled back, at the same time receiving the command to heel. If the dog persists in running forward it may be lightly tapped on the nose with a light switch. As the lessons progress the dog will soon learn to jaunt along beside its companion.

Every puppy must be housebroken. While in the house the puppy should be carefully watched for signs of uneasiness; this is a warning to take it out. After a while the dog will learn that by going to the door it will be taken out and the owner should always respond by taking the dog out immediately. Of course, sooner or later, the puppy is bound to have an accident, and then it must be shown what it has done and severely scolded. If, however, the dog persists in this behavior, it should be punished, providing the punishment can be associated with the misbehavior. With a little care the dog can be regulated to go out at certain hours. It should have this opportunity at least twice, and better four times a day, one of which is the last thing at night.

Below, left: **A Poodle learns 'Lie Down.'** *Below, right:* **A puppy's first lesson will be housebreaking.** *Facing page:* **A Pomeranian.**

SAMOYED

The Samoyed is best known as a sled dog, working hard in the Far North. The Samoyed is believed to have originated in Mongolia and was later transported to Siberia. Developed as an all-around guard, hunting, and sled dog, the Samoyed was a valued companion to the nomadic Samoyed tribes as they roamed around northern Asia.

The Samoyed became known to the rest of the world after famous polar explorers such as Roald Amundsen and Fridtjof Jansen used the dogs on their expeditions. Almost all modern Samoyeds outside the Soviet Union are the descendents of the polar expedition dogs.

The Samoyed is more than just a sled dog, however; it is also an extremely beautiful dog. It has several outstanding features, probably the most distinctive of which is its thick, white, double coat of hair, which includes a large ruff around the neck. Second is its full, bushy tail which the Samoyed carries forward over its body. And third is the distinctive Samoyed mouth which turns up to form an especially happy grin. These three features, together with the Samoyed's triangular, erect ears and dark, almond-shaped eyes, give the dog a sparkling and attractive appearance.

The Samoyed's thick, white coat (which can also be cream colored or grayish yellow) is made up of two layers: a harsh, long outer coat, and a dense, woolly undercoat. Its double-thickness makes it well-suited for the Arctic cold and also insulates it from summer heat.

The Samoyed is still used today in the Arctic to guard reindeer and pull sleds. Even in the absence of reindeer, however, the Samoyed makes a good watchdog, and, like its ancestors, a good companion. The Samoyed watchdog is not a vicious one, but rather one that operates with intelligence and alertness. The Samoyed is also a very loyal and friendly dog with an especially playful nature. Fortunately, with its happy demeanor, the Samoyed has little difficulty attracting human playmates.

Below: A Samoyed puppy. *Right:* The sparkling eyes, erect ears, 'grinning' mouth and general look of animation create what is known as the Samoyed expression.

SCHIPPERKE

Schipperke means little captain in Flemish, and that is exactly what the Schipperke was several centuries ago. Originating in Flanders, the Schipperke once guarded canal barges and hurried the horses that pulled them. Although its exact lineage is unknown, the Schipperke is believed to have descended from a black sheep dog called the Leauvenaar which is now extinct. In 1885, the Schipperke's popularity soared almost overnight, when it became the pet of the Queen of Belgium. A few years later, the Schipperke was brought to the United States, but it never gained as much favor here as it did in its native homeland.

The Schipperke looks a little like a northern sled dog. It has a short, thick-set build, a deep, broad chest, and very muscular hindquarters. Its thick, double coat is made up of a dense, harsh outercoat of straight hair, and an undercoat of soft, fine hair. The coat is especially dense and long around the neck and hindquarters, forming a ruff and culottes respectively. The Schipperke's face, however, looks more like that of a fox than of a northern sled dog: It is wide, narrowing at the eyes, and ends in a medium-length muzzle. Also like a fox, it has small, erect ears that are high-set and triangular. The Schipperke's tail is usually nonexistent or docked.

A unique personality goes along with the small black dog's singular appearance. In the fifteenth century the Schipperke was described as 'the incarnation of the devil' — perhaps because it is very restless, darting here and there, and curious, poking its sharp, pointed nose into every aspect of family life and expressing its opinion by barking shrilly and raising its ruff. The Schipperke is affectionate, gentle and extremely patient with children, but a little snobbish and jealous of other pets, and suspicious of strangers. It is a very hardy and energetic dog that is generally easy to raise. It is long lived, usually living to be 15 and 16 years old. A Scottish Schipperke lived to be 21 years old.

These pages: **The ever curious Schipperke makes an excellent and faithful little watchdog.**

SCOTTISH TERRIER

Often called by the name *Scottie* the Scottish Terrier is a small dog that thinks of itself as a giant. Nobody bosses the Scottie around because this dog demands to be treated like a king. The plucky little Scottie almost never shies away from a contest of wills — even if the opponent is its owner.

The Scottish Terrier was raised in the Scottish highlands in the 1800s. Because it came from a rocky area around Aberdeen, Scotland, the Scottie has also been called the Aberdeen Terrier. The Scottie's family tree includes many cousins — the Skye, Cairn and West Highland White Terriers, for example — because of the enormous amount of interbreeding that took place at that time. The Scottish Terrier, however, is the oldest of the Highland Terriers.

The Scottie was originally developed to pursue foxes ferrets, badgers and other pest animals into their underground retreats. It was brought to the United States in 1883, and gained tremendous fame when Franklin Roosevelt took his beloved Scottish Terrier, *Fala*, to the White House. Since then, the Scottie has become both a popular pet and show dog.

Although Scottish Terrier puppies are adorable, the adult Scottie sometimes has been referred to as a bit dour-looking. Perhaps it is the shaggy eyebrows and the bewhiskered face on a rather longish head. In any case, the Scottie is a small dog with a strong, but chunky, body on short legs. It has small, upright ears and an undocked tail. Its double coat consists of a dense undercoat of short, soft hair and a dense outercoat of harsh, wiry hair. Most Scotties are black, but there are also Scotties of other colors, such as wheat, steel grey and brindle.

The independent Scottie has a distinct rollicking gait, which somewhat reflects its high self-esteem. Although the jaunty Scottie can be aggressive with other pets, it is very sensitive to the moods of humans, particularly its owner's. Sometimes described as a one-person dog, the self-assured Scottie is best paired with an owner who won't take personally the Scottie's occasional, but trying, fits of stubbornness.

The Scottish Terrier *(above and below)* is known for its independent, feisty temperament. *Right:* A Scottie puppy.

SHAR-PEI

Although the Shar-Pei is listed in the *Guinness Book of World Records* as the rarest dog in the world, it may not have that distinction for long because interest in the breed is steadily increasing. It was in 1947 that the Shar-Pei almost became extinct and earned its place in the *Guinness Book*, when the tax on dogs in the People's Republic of China rose so high that few people could afford to keep a pet, and the Chinese Government ordered all dogs destroyed. However, dog lovers in Hong Kong saved the Shar-Pei from extinction.

The origin of this unusual dog is unknown, though it is thought it may have descended from the Chow Chow because they both have purple tongues. Art works survive from the Han Dynasty, 206 BC to 220 AD, which depict a dog resembling the Shar-Pei, but where it came from is in question. Some authorities suggest the Northern Province of China or Tibet, while others say the Shar-Pei may have come from the Southern Province near the South China Sea.

The Shar-Pei's intelligence was greatly valued, and if this quality was missing the dog was slaughtered and eaten. It was also known for its versatility. As a fighting dog in the ring, the Shar-Pei may have been the first animal athlete drugged to make it more aggressive and ferocious, for it naturally has a sweet and loving disposition. The Shar-Pei's loose skin made it hard for its opponent to get a good grip on its body. This gentle dog was also used to hunt wild boar and served as a guard dog of family and flock. Today, in the United States, the Shar-Pei has become almost exclusively a cherished companion, which probably suits it just fine.

The price is high for a good Shar-Pei, as a female in season will only attract certain members of her own breed (never those of other breeds), and so the right dog must be found or no puppies will be forthcoming. An advantage, though, is that Shar-Pei puppies house-train themselves.

The Shar-Pei looks as if its skin is several sizes too big for its body. It is strongly built and weighs between 35 and 45 pounds. Coat colors are black, light and dark fawn, cream, red, sable, and chocolate, all self colors preferred with a blue-grey muzzle. The ears are set high and folded so that they point toward the eyes, while the tail curls over the back.

Though not yet registered by the AKC, the Shar-Pei is a purebred dog, and the Shar-Pei Club of America was formed to adopt a breed standard, so registration may soon be forthcoming.

***These pages:* Once almost extinct, the unusual-looking Shar-Pei has gained popularity in recent years.**

Below: The soft, wrinkled skin of the Shar-Pei makes it look like a cuddly stuffed animal.

SHETLAND SHEEPDOG

Like the Collie that it closely resembles, the Shetland Sheepdog can trace its roots back to the Border Collie of Scotland. The Sheltie, as the breed is affectionately known, was transported to the Shetland Islands, where it was crossed with small, intelligent, long-haired breeds. Subsequent crosses were occasionally made with the Collie.

This agile and sturdy dog stands 13 to 16 inches. The Shetland Sheepdog's chest is deep, its back level and strongly muscled, and its thighs broad and muscular. The long wedged-shaped head is crowned with two perky ears. The shape of the head, combined with the set of the ears and the placement and color of the eyes, creates an alert, intelligent expression.

The Shetland Sheepdog's most distinctive feature is its dense coat, which consists of an outercoat of long, straight, harsh hair and a short, furry undercoat. The undercoat is so dense that it makes the entire coat stand out. The hair on the face, tips of the ears, and feet is smooth. The abundant mane and frill are particularly impressive on males. The Sheltie's coat is black, blue merle or sable, marked with varying amounts of white and/or tan.

This intensely loyal dog is affectionate and responsive to its owner, but may be reserved with strangers. Its gentle nature makes it a good family dog. Although the Sheltie is a small dog, it was bred to be a working dog and therefore enjoys a lot of activity.

Below: **The Shetland Sheepdog's expression is alert, intelligent and gentle.** *Right:* **An absolutely adorable bundle of fluff — a Sheltie puppy.**

SHIH TZU

The Shih Tzu was developed in China, but its ultimate place of origin is Tibet. One theory holds that the breed is descended from the Lhasa Apsos of Tibet, which were bred as pampered pets of the upper classes. On occasion, Lhasa Apsos were sent to Imperial China as gifts or tribute. Its likely that once in China, the Lhasa Apsos were bred with Pekingese (or that breed's ancestors). This cross produced the shorter muzzle, domed head and shorter legs of the Shih Tzu. In turn, the introduction of Shih Tzu blood may have given the Pekingese its heavy coat. In addition, Pugs and Tibetan Spaniels probably played a part in the development of this noble little canine. Shih Tzu means little lion in Chinese, and it is believed that the Shih Tzu and its ancestors were the models for the Tibetan lion dogs that play a prominent part in Chinese art and folklore.

The Shih Tzu is a very active, lively and alert dog, with a distinctly arrogant carriage. Befitting its noble heritage, the Shih Tzu is proud of bearing, carrying its head high and its tail gaily as it walks.

For a toy dog, the Shih Tzu is fairly substantial, ideally weighing 12 to 15 pounds and measuring 9 to 10 ½ inches at the withers. The dog has a broad and deep chest, well rounded and muscular hindquarters, and short, well boned, muscular legs. The legs appear massive because of the thick coat of hair. Its head is broad and round, and wide between the eyes, with a square and short muzzle.

The Shih Tzu's coat is luxurious, long and dense, with a woolly undercoat. Any color is permissible, but the coat should not be curly. Some owners gather the hair on top of the head in a bow, and this practice is even permitted for show dogs.

The American Kennel Club recognized the Shih Tzu in 1969, and the breed found immediate acceptance owing to its charming personality.

These pages: **Its even-tempered disposition and beautiful coat have made the Shih Tzu one of the most popular toy breeds.**

SIBERIAN HUSKY

The Siberian Husky is probably best known as a winning sled dog in Alaskan sled-dog races. Although it did not begin participating in the races until the early 1900s, the Siberian Husky has always been a sled dog, capable of traveling great distances at a fairly good speed. Because of its light weight, it has a reputation for being much faster than many other northern sled dogs.

Perhaps dating back to the time when a land bridge connected Siberia with Alaska, the Siberian Husky was developed in Siberia by the Chukchi, a seminomadic people who valued it as a sled dog, a companion and a guard. Although related to the Alaskan Malamute, the Eskimo Dog (a native dog of the Arctic Coastal regions) and the Samoyed, the Siberian Husky was kept pure for hundreds of years in Siberia. In addition to use by the Chukchi, Russian explorers used packs of the dog on their many journeys charting the Siberian coastline. The dog was especially adept at carrying light loads at very low temperatures. It was brought to Alaska in 1909 for a sled-dog race and did so well that it soon became a familiar sight. It was recognized by the American Kennel Club in 1930, and by the United Kennel Club — under the name Arctic Husky — in 1932.

The graceful and quick Siberian Husky is medium-sized with a body a little longer than it is tall. Its lithe build includes a deep chest, a strong back and very muscled hindquarters. It has a wedge-shaped head with a tapering muzzle and erect, triangular ears. Its almond-shaped eyes (which can be brown or blue or one of each color) are set at a slant, giving the dog a friendly and mischievous look. Its bushy and foxlike tail is carried in an arch over the back.

The coat of the Siberian Husky is thick and soft and most attractive-looking. Of medium length, the furry, double coat consists of a straight, smooth-lying outercoat and a soft, dense undercoat. Although the color of the coat comes in all hues, from black to pure white, most Siberian Huskies are grey, tan or black. Giving some of the dogs an especially eye-catching appearance are striking white markings on the head, resembling a cap, mask or spectacles.

This intelligent dog is by nature gentle and friendly. It is extremely trustworthy and a good family dog. Its independent nature often leads it to wander, however, and thus it does not always make a good watchdog.

Although it sheds heavily in the spring, the Siberian Husky is unlike many dense-coated breeds in that it is generally free of unpleasant odors. Bred as a working dog, the Siberian Husky needs lots of exercise; inactivity or confinement will often result in neurotic behavior. If given exercise, the Siberian Husky can adapt to city life, but it is happiest in the country where it can play with a companion outdoors, taking particular pleasure in pulling sleds or other small, wheeled vehicles.

These fluffy Siberian Husky puppies *(these pages)* will grow up to be friendly, agreeable companions.

SILKY TERRIER

Once known as the Sydney Silky, this toy dog originated in Sydney, Australia in the early 1900s. The Silky was developed from a cross between the Australian terrier — which was a descendant of the Skye terrier — and the Yorkshire terrier from England. The Skye terrier is probably responsible for the Silky's silken coat.

Because it is a very small dog, the Australians primarily enjoyed the Silky as a pet, and, on farms, used the dog to kill rats and snakes. Perhaps due to the long distance between countries, the Silky made a rather late entrance into the United States and Canada, not making an appearance until the 1950s. It made up for lost time rather quickly, however, gaining recognition from the American Kennel Club in 1959, and becoming one of the 45 most popular breeds by the 1970s.

The Silky's outstanding characteristic is its silky, fine coat. The flat coat lays very long on the body, with a profuse amount of hair on the top of the head, and shorter amounts on the face, ears, and legs (from the knees to the feet). The hair is parted exactly down the head and over the back to the root of the tail. The glossy coat is usually tan and/or various shades of blue, such as blue grey, silver blue or pigeon blue. Usually, the Silky's topknot of hair is silver grey or tan.

This debonair dog stands only 9 to 10 inches tall and has a body that is a little longer than its height. The Silky has a wedge-shaped head with a flat skull that is not very wide between its high-set, erect ears. The Silky's eyes are small and piercing, giving it a very alert appearance. Completing the picture is the Silky's docked tail, which, although high-set and carried upright, does not have enough hair to form a plume.

The Silky is generally a very friendly and responsible dog and is still popular in Australia as a city pet. It is also a very active, spirited and energetic dog, however, and very much likes doing things in its own way at all times. It especially objects to variations in routines. It is well suited for being an excellent watchdog because it is mentally and physically quick, very vocal and usually aggressive towards other animals and strangers. What the Silky lacks in size, it makes up for in feistiness and independence.

SMOOTH FOX TERRIER

The Smooth Fox Terrier is one of the most cosmopolitan dogs in the world. It achieved this distinction during the colonial expansion period of the British Empire. Being an ever-faithful companion of the British, Smooth Fox Terriers accompanied their English masters throughout the world as they staked out and claimed new territories for the British throne.

Now best known as a pet, the Smooth Fox Terrier was originally valued as a hunting dog. In particular, the Smooth Fox Terrier was used by mounted fox hunters to pursue foxes and dig them out of their holes. The Smooth Fox Terrier is still considered a sporting dog, but it is found more often performing in dog shows than out in the field.

Although many people could not physically describe the Smooth Fox Terrier if asked to do so, almost everyone would recognize the trademark dog that is on many old record labels. The trademark, from 'His Master's Voice' records, shows a Smooth Fox Terrier listening into an old-fashioned gramophone. The dog pictured has button ears folding over the top of its head, and a smooth, sleek coat that is predominantly white with a few markings of black on the body. Other physical characteristics of the Smooth Fox Terrier are small, dark eyes and an erect, docked tail. Many Smooth Fox Terriers have a black head with a tan mask covering the eyes and cheeks, and some Smooth Fox Terriers are completely white. At one time, the Smooth Fox Terrier was considered a different coat variety, but the same breed, as the Wiry Fox Terrier, and vice versa. Now, however, the two dogs are recognized as two distinct breeds and not two coat varieties of a single breed.

These pages: **The Silky Terrier has the typical terrier personality — alert, friendly and spirited.**

The smart-looking Smooth Fox Terrier is a boisterous dog not well-suited to a person who loves peace and quiet. Friendly, and very energetic, the Smooth Fox Terrier does best with an active family or owner — people who prefer to take their dog with them rather than leave it sitting home alone. The Smooth Fox Terrier loves playing with children, especially those who include the dog in ball games or games which require the retrieval of objects. Like most terriers, the Smooth Fox Terrier can be very aggressive towards other dogs, and males especially are likely to engage in dog fights. On the positive side, its aggressiveness, coupled with a tendency to be vocal, makes the Smooth Fox Terrier an excellent watchdog.

SOFT-COATED WHEATEN TERRIER

The Soft-Coated Wheaten Terrier is exactly as its name suggests: soft-coated and of a wheaten color. Although terriers with soft coats have been bred in Ireland for the last several centuries, written documentation of the breeds is almost nonexistent. As it is, the Wheaten Terrier is one of only a few terrier breeds to have a soft coat.

Like most terriers originating in Ireland, the Soft-Coated Wheaten Terrier was developed as an all-purpose farm dog. Usually belonging to farmers and laborers, the dog was expected to guard the house, watch the animals and be a sporting or playful companion to the master and the children. The Wheaten Terrier was officially recognized by Ireland in 1937, and by England in 1943. By 1946, the Wheaten had arrived in the United States, but it did not receive recognition from the American Kennel Club until 1973.

The sturdy, medium-sized Wheaten Terrier has a very angular profile. Its solid, well-proportioned body is very similar to that of the Kerry Blue Terrier, but the Wheaten's head is both broader and shorter. It also has the typical docked terrier tail, small, dark eyes, and cute, little button ears. The most distinctive feature, however, is the Wheaten's coat, which is not only a clear, wheaten color, but also soft and wavy. The coat is usually trimmed only to show off the dog's outline, although occasionally the fringe around the ears is also trimmed.

The Wheaten is a happy dog that enjoys being a companion to adults or children. Its cheerful personality makes it an ideal dog for families, especially because the Wheaten gets along well with other pets. Unlike many terriers, the Wheaten displays very little aggressive behavior. When given enough grooming (so its coat doesn't get matted) and sufficient exercise, the Wheaten is truly a wonderful dog that is as eager to please as it is to love.

SPINONE ITALIANO

The Spinone Italiano's gentle eyes, with an almost human expression, peer through ruffled eyebrows. A moustache and a beard decorate its friendly face. The Italian Spinone is a solid, sturdy dog with strong bones, but still on the slender side. It stands 23 to 27.5 inches tall and weighs between 62 and 81.5 pounds. Its thick, wiry, slightly curly white coat protects the Spinone Italiano from thorny bushes and icy streams, for it hunts equally well on land or in the water. In summer, the coat thins and the dog is comfortable in the dry, warm Italian climate. The Spinone Italiano wears its tail docked so it won't get caught in the brambles.

The Spinone Italiano originated in the 1600s in the Bresse area of France, and later became established in the Piedmont area of Italy. His ancestors include the French Griffon, French and German Pointers, Porcelaine, Barbet, and Korthals Griffon. This crossbreeding produced one of the best pointing griffons, with subtle nose and soft mouth, which made the Spinone Italiano popular with all classes of hunters for all types of hunting until the French Revolution, when the breed went into a period of decline, rising again in popularity only in the late 1900s. Today, it continues to be a sportsman's favorite, especially in Italy. When the hunt is over, the Spinone Italiano makes an excellent pet, since it is intelligent, good-natured

and clean. The American Kennel Club welcomes the Spinone Italiano in the Miscellaneous Class at its shows.

It has been said this adaptable dog gets its name from the Italian word *spino*, meaning 'thorn' or 'bramble,' which refers to its coat with its thick, thorny fur. *Spinone* translates into 'griffon,' which is related to griffin, and has several different meanings, the most pertinent being 'any of several varieties of the Brussels griffon, also called wire-haired pointing griffon.'

STAFFORDSHIRE BULL TERRIER

When bullbaiting was made illegal in the early nineteenth century, the more bloodthirsty members of society turned to dogfighting as their new source of entertainment. Since strong, agile dogs with lots of spunk and tenacity put on the best show, such a dog was developed.

Its distant ancestors were the Bulldog and Mastiff, bred down from 100 to 120 pounds to 90 pounds. The first 60-pound specimen was known as the Bulldog Terrier and the Bull and Terrier. It was crossed with the English Terrier (now extinct), and the dog which this produced, weighing between 30 and 45 pounds, became the Staffordshire Bull Terrier — named for the miners of Staffordshire, England, who were great fans of these fights.

This ugly, pugnacious dog was a natural fighter and was also renowned as a ratter. When dogfighting was outlawed, the miners of Staffordshire continued to breed pit dogs for secret matches long after dogfights were declared illegal. Because the Staffordshire Bull Terrier can be a devoted and charming companion, if raised with strength and affection, the breed was saved from extinction. Courageous in battle, this dog will give up its his life in defense of his owner.

The Staffordshire Bull Terrier stands 14 to 16 inches tall at the shoulder. Its head is short and broad with a pronounced stop, and its body is well rounded with a short, smooth coat of red, fawn, white, black, blue or any of these colors with white. The dog's front legs are straight and wide apart, and its hind legs are muscular, with hocks let down and stifles well bent. The medium-length tail is undocked and carried low.

The Staffordshire Bull Terrier was recognized by the British Kennel Club in the mid 1930s and became a part of the American Kennel Club stud book in 1974.

TIBETAN SPANIEL

Early versions of the Tibetan Spaniel existed in prehistoric time, as proven by scientific digs of ancient dwelling places. There are also depictions of Tibetan Spaniel-type dogs in ancient Eastern art. Tibetan Spaniels appear in numerous medieval pieces of art, the oldest being a Chinese painting from the 1400s.

In the seventeenth century, when Tibet adopted the Buddhist religion, these small golden dogs became known as 'little lions.' Trailing behind the lamas in the monasteries, they were thought to resemble the lion of the Lord Buddha, which followed at his heels like a faithful dog. As this lion represented Buddha's power over violence and aggression, the diminutive dogs were highly regarded by the deeply religious and peace-loving Tibetans.

The practice of presenting these small dogs to high-ranking dignitaries in China and other Buddhist countries became popular as a mark of esteem, and the grateful recipients returned the favor by presenting their lion dogs to the Tibetan lamas and important officials. This canine exchange continued until as late as 1908, and the crossings that followed produced a more refined Tibetan Spaniel.

The Buddhist religion was central to the coming to prominence of the Tibetan Spaniel, as well as to related breeds. (The Tibetan

continued on page 178

Right: **The Soft-Coated Wheaten Terrier has a well balanced, moderately long head profusely covered with hair that falls forward, shading its eyes.**

An active and happy animal, the Soft-Coated Wheaten Terrier *(above)* is one of the old, traditional breeds of Ireland.

Spaniel is either the progenitor or the cousin of several of today's breeds, such as the Japanese Chin, the Lhasa Apso, the Papillon, the Pug, and the Pekinese.) Because Buddhists believe in the doctrine of reincarnation, they believed that in the past they might have been animals and might be so again in the future. This tenet, along with the warm feelings the little lions engendered as peace symbols, and a belief that there are no real spiritual differences between man and dog, encouraged kind treatment to all animals in Tibet. Buddhists placed clay figurines of Tibetan Spaniels within early Chinese tombs, which, they believed, would result in service from the dogs in the lives to come.

These small animals were considered useful also as watchdogs, for during the day they would watch the surrounding countryside from positions on top of the monastery walls, and at the approach of visitors, or wolves to the flocks grazing below, would commence a shrill, continuous barking. They were backed up by a huge Tibetan Mastiff, as well as by monks and concerned shepherds.

Tibetan Spaniels made their way to England in the late 1800s, but arrived in America only in the 1960s. The Tibetan Spaniel Club of America was formed, with 14 charter members, in January 1971, and the breed was accepted for AKC registration on 1 January 1984.

This extremely intelligent, good-natured, affectionate, family-oriented, friendly dog has a distinctive personality, said to be catlike. The Tibetan Spaniel is distinguished by its hare feet, and cat feet are a fault. It weighs between nine and 15 pounds and measures about 10 inches at the withers. A plumed tail carried over the back is a characteristic. All colors are allowed, but golden is preferred.

One of the benefits of this breed is its total naturalness. It is presented in the show ring in an entirely unaltered condition, and any alteration by artificial means, such as clipping or trimming, is so severely penalized as to effectively eliminate the dog from the competition. Only occasional brushing and bathing are required.

TIBETAN TERRIER

The Tibetan Terrier is primarily a pet. It may also serve, however, as a guard dog, because it is protective of its family and their possessions, and will sound the alarm with its loud bark if anyone approaches its territory. This small, shaggy dog, which resembles the Old English Sheepdog, may also try to help round up any farm animals that stray.

Although called a terrier, it is not a terrier at all, and has neither the disposition nor the inclination to dig in the earth, as is characteristic of that type of dog. Both of the names by which the breed is known in Tibet — 'Luck Bringer' and 'Holy Dog' — seemed inappropriate in the dog world outside Tibet, so the dog was dubbed a terrier, because it is the same size as that group of dogs.

Having lived and survived for as many as 2000 years in one of the world's most inhospitable climates, Tibetan Terriers are very healthy. In the high mountains and deep valleys of Tibet, it is windy and icy cold in the winter and hot and humid in the summer. Yet faced with the worst blizzard the Tibetan Terrier keeps warm owing to its double coat, which includes fur mask and fur toe covers, as well as snowshoe feet to help it walk on the snow. In the middle of a hot summer day the Tibetan Terrier will relax and take a siesta.

Like the Tibetan Spaniel and the Lhasa Apso, the Tibetan Terrier was originally raised by the lamas in the holy city of Lhasa. These good luck dogs were never sold, because the Buddhist religion forbids selling living things, but also because no family would sell part of their luck out of fear of losing all their luck. The dogs were given away, though, in gratitude for favors. Dr ARH Greig, a physician who treated a Tibetan's sick wife in India in the 1920s, was presented with a Tibetan Terrier by the grateful husband. Dr Greig started a breeding kennel in India and when she returned to England she founded the famous Lamleh Kennel there.

The first official Tibetan Terrier brought to the United States came from the Lamleh Kennel. Dr and Mrs Henry S Murphy of Great Falls, Virginia, purchased a pedigreed London Kennel Club dog, and since then the breed has become popular all over the United States and in Canada. The American Kennel Club recognized the Tibetan Terrier on 1 May 1973, and admitted the breed to regular show classification in the Non-Sporting Group at AKC shows on 3 October 1973.

The Tibetan Terrier weighs between 17 and 30 pounds and is 14 to 16 inches tall at the shoulders. It is good-natured, intelligent and affectionate, but wary of strangers. The Tibetan Terrier's tail is carried in a gay curl over its back, and often there is a kink near the tip.

TOY POODLE

Although the Standard Poodle was first on the scene, the Miniature and Toy varieties made their entrance soon after. They were developed from smaller specimens and are identical to the largest poodle, except in size.

The Toy Poodle was probably never used to hunt ducks and more likely became a pet dog at once. Its beauty, intelligence, trainability and attractive personality (qualities shared by all three sizes) make it a joy to own. The Poodle is sensitive, however, so will not accept heavy-handed training.

The Poodle does not shed its hair, and to keep this stylish dog looking its most chic, it needs to go to the beauty salon about every six weeks. Happy in an apartment, this tiny charmer enjoys trotting beside his owner in the park, learning tricks and just being an adored pet.

WEIMARANER

Nicknamed the Gray Ghost, the Weimaraner has a striking appearance. Its powerfully built body is covered with a short, sleek coat of grey — grey rose, mouse-grey or silver-grey — and its eyes are generally of an amber hue, or sometimes blue or green. Partially because of its deep chest and straight back, the Weimaraner has a very aristocratic look and a well-balanced stance at all times. It is exceptionally graceful and silent when hunting, and it is at this time that the illusion of a grey ghost is most apparent.

Originally developed in the nineteenth century by German nobles of the Court of Weimar, the Weimaraner was the result of ancient Bloodhound stock being crossed with German Short-haired Pointers. The new dogs were first used to hunt big game, such as deer and bears, and then were trained as bird dogs and retrievers. In Germany, the dogs were the favorite gundogs of the Weimar Court, and were often referred to as Weimar Pointers.

The Weimar Court valued the dog for its nose, intelligence, courage and speed. In fact, the Weimar Court regarded the dog so highly that it jealously guarded it and made it almost impossible to obtain outside the court. Eventually, however, the dog did leave the court, and as it gained in popularity throughout Germany, several rules were established regarding its breeding. Probably the most important rule was that only members of the German Weimaraner Club could buy the dog. In 1929, an American named Howard Knight joined the club and brought two dogs to the United States. Knight then founded his own Weimaraner Club, and, in 1943, the Weimaraner gained recognition from the American Kennel Club.

Perhaps due to its hunting heritage, the Weimaraner is an assertive and bold dog, usually requiring obedience training. Without training, the Weimaraner can be very stubborn and impetuous, and extremely difficult to manage. It is also better off in the country than in the city because it needs lots of room to run. The Weimaraner detests being shut up in an apartment, waiting for its owner to return home from work. Of course this situation will not last long because the Weimaraner will soon rebel by being destructive.

Despite its somewhat difficult traits, the Weimaraner is an intelligent and friendly dog, making for a very good companion. And, when with a family that is capable of being in command, the Weimaraner is loving and devoted.

Right: **With its fine aristocratic features, the Weimaraner is the picture of grace, alertness, speed and stamina.**

WEST HIGHLAND WHITE TERRIER

Often referred to as the Westie, the West Highland White Terrier is related to the Cairn Terrier in a most unusual way. At one time, if the Cairn Terrier had a white puppy in its litter, that puppy was considered undesirable and destroyed. Then someone decided to spare the white puppies, and from those dogs the West Highland White Terrier was developed.

For many years, the Westie was primarily bred by the estate of Malcolm of Poltalloch in Argyllshire, located in the Western Highlands of Scotland. The Malcolm family had many dogs, some of which traced back to the time of King James I of England. The family's breeding of the West Highland White Terrier was very successful, and, in the early 1900s, the dog arrived in the United States. It received American recognition in 1908.

The Westie is a very compact-looking dog with short legs and a short, broad head. The Westie ears are small and pointed, and the eyes are dark and alert. It has an erect tail which is undocked. The Westie's distinctive white coat is made up of two layers: a soft, furry undercoat and a straight, hard outercoat. Abundant hair covers the Westie's face and head, with shorter hair on the neck and shoulders. Like a black button on a snowball, the Westie's jet-black nose (which is pink at birth) contrasts nicely with its pure white coat, the only color it comes in.

Although the Westie makes a good watchdog — it is quite vocal when upset — the Westie's personality can best be described as light-hearted, outgoing and sunny. It is at home in any setting, but seems happiest when with a few well-chosen friends, human or canine. All in all, this hardy-looking, little dog has abundant charm, making it one of the most beloved of all terriers.

A small dog, the West Highland White Terrier *(these pages)* **has a spunky and friendly personality.**

Below: A family of Westies. These happy, self-reliant dogs make good family pets.

WHIPPET

Greatly resembling a miniature greyhound, the Whippet has a lean, muscular form which enables it to run close to speeds of 35 miles an hour. So fast is the medium-sized Whippet that it is often referred to as the 'poor man's racehorse.'

Whippets were developed almost 150 years ago by breeders in northern England. Crossing small English Greyhounds with terriers, the object was to produce a superior 'snap dog' — a term used for dogs which chased rabbits in an enclosure and then 'snapped them up.' The hope was also that the new breed would excel in rat-killing competitions, which it did. Later, to give the Whippet an even sleeker appearance, the dog was bred with Italian Greyhounds. In 1891, the breed was officially recognized by the Kennel Club of England.

In addition to its streamlined body, the Whippet is distinguished by its prominent ears, which fold over and back against its neck when racing. It also has a deep chest (rather than wide), and a stomach which is tucked up. The Whippet's long tail is normally carried under the body. English Whippets are slightly smaller than American-bred Whippets. All Whippets, however, regardless of size or origin, have a close, smooth coat, usually in the colors of grey, tan, or white.

Despite its penchant for racing, the Whippet is generally considered a quiet and even-tempered dog. It is highly intelligent, extremely responsive and affectionate. As it is seldom seen making ungainly movements, the Whippet is described by many as the epitome of grace and elegance.

Below: **Similar in appearance to the Greyhound, the Whippet is smaller, more refined and gentler.** *Right:* **A Whippet at rest.**

YORKSHIRE TERRIER

Strutting around with an air of importance, the little Yorkshire Terrier proudly displays its straight and silky coat, which is sometimes so long that it sweeps the ground. Parted on the back from its nose to its slightly plumed tail, the distinctive-looking steel blue grey with golden tan coat includes a topknot of hair, which is fashionably tied with a ribbon in the center of the Yorkie's head. With a glint in its eye, the intelligent little Yorkie seems to know just how stylish a picture it presents.

Like the Toy Poodle, the toy Yorkshire Terrier is now something of a status symbol: Good Yorkies can be very, very expensive. And yet, the Yorkshire Terrier was originally a worker's dog. Developed in Yorkshire and Lancashire during the Victorian period, the Yorkshire Terrier was bred by English weavers who wanted a dog bold enough to kill rats but small enough to be carried in the pocket. Weighing only four to seven pounds, the Yorkshire Terrier fit the bill perfectly. Over time, the little Yorkshire Terrier became the darling of all classes, and travelled to the United States with some of its owners in the late nineteenth century.

The Yorkshire Terrier's lineage is not exactly known, but it appears to be a mixture of several terrier breeds, some of which are extinct. It is mostly closely related to the Skye and Dandie Dinmont Terriers, and perhaps the Maltese breed as well. Physically, the Yorkshire Terrier has a body resembling most terriers: compact, short legs, and an upright carriage. It has a small head with a flat top and flat V-shaped ears. The eyes are dark with dark rims, and the nose is black. Unlike many dogs, it has round feet with black nails. The Yorkshire tail is docked, with a long fall of hair.

Looks aside, the energetic and assertive Yorkie makes a good watchdog and family pet. It is easily trained and gets along well with children of all ages, and even other pets (including cats). Care must be taken around the tiny Yorkie, however, because the fragile dog can be killed by the hard slam of a door. The Yorkshire is a good apartment dog because it needs little exercise — in fact, its favorite exercise is probably jumping up on its owner's lap. The Yorkshire loves to be pampered, and some say it's the ultimate pampered pet.

Yorkshire puppies *(pages 188–191)* are born black and tan, with an intermingling of black hair in the tan. As they mature, their coats grow longer, and the black hair lightens to a dark steel blue. *Page 192:* The Bouvier des Flandres.